ANGEL BY YOUR SIDE

ANGEL BY YOUR SIDE

Inspirational Stories of Amazing Coincidences

Marilyn Frazer

Angel by Your Side
Inspirational Stories of Amazing Coincidences

ISBN: 978-0-578-93951-3 (paperback)
Library of Congress Control Number: 2021913535

Published by
Marilyn Frazer
Orlando, Florida
www.marilynfrazer.com

Cover design by Grace Bolyard Quest, thegracequest@gmail.com

Book Shepherd Ann Narcisian Videan, ANVidean.com

Contents

Introduction		1
1	A Farewell Dinner	4
2	The Pool Party	7
3	Does God Exist?	9
4	Stopping to Smell the Roses	12
5	A Miracle For Christopher	15
6	A Member of the Audience	22
7	One Foggy Night	25
8	One More Time	28
9	The Treasure Chest	30
10	"2-5-8"	33
11	His Anniversary Gift	35
12	Jesse	37
13	Dorothy's Spirit	43
14	Mom's Dream	46
15	The Killer Mint	48
16	Flight 191	50
17	Noelle	56
18	Double Take	58
19	It's a Small World	60
20	My Sister's Story	62
21	With Love From Russia	64
22	Cosmic Coincidence	65

23	The Number 10 Bus	68
24	Angel in China	71
25	Butterfly Wings	76
	She Played to the Dragonfly	77
26	Reaching Across the Bar	78
27	A Punch in the Gut	81
28	Never Really Lost	83
29	When Time Stood Still	88
30	Cruising Along	90
31	Heavenly Music	95
32	A Gift From Above	97
33	A Question Answered	99
34	The Legend of the Dish	102
35	Why Me?	104
36	A Chance Meeting	106
37	As Grandpa Lay Dying	108
38	Denali	110
39	Wait For Me	113
40	The Man We Called Angel	116
41	A Mystical Experience	118
42	Do Not Be Afraid	122
43	Flying High	125
44	Midnight Shift	128
45	A Light from Above	129

Request for Review

...a still, small voice
of an angel...

To my family,
my inspiration.

Introduction

Beneath the Wings of Angels

Mark Twain was born in 1835 on the day of the appearance of Halley's Comet, and died in 1910, the day it next appeared. In 1909, he predicted this would happen when he said: "I came in with Halley's Comet in 1835. It is coming again next year, and I expect to go out with it."

Amazing coincidence?

Violet Jessop was an Irish immigrant born in Argentina, who moved to England with her family when she was sixteen years old and lived to the ripe old age of 83 years. A long life considering that Jessop managed to cheat death on several occasions, surviving against all odds. She worked as an ocean liner stewardess and amazingly survived three separate disasters on huge ocean liners, including the sinking of the *Titanic*. The three ships were the largest and most luxurious boats of the early twentieth century, but all experienced horrible accidents.

Violet's first job was in 1908 with the Royal Mail Line on the *Orinoco*. Then she transferred to The *RMS Olympic,* which made her maiden voyage on October 20, 1910. On June 14, 1911, the *Olympic* collided with the cruiser *HMS Hawke*. At the time of the accident, the *Olympic* was the largest civilian liner in the world. Although the *Olympic* was heavily damaged and flooded when it crashed, it was able to make it back to Southampton, England. Violet survived the crash unharmed. The *Olympic's* Captain Smith went on to command the *Titanic* on her ill-fated maiden voyage the following year.

On April 10, 1912, Violet boarded the *RMS Titanic*. Four days later, the boat hit an iceberg and sank in the North Atlantic. During the sinking, Violet was asked to proceed to the lifeboats and set an example for the people who did not speak English and were having a hard time following directions. She boarded the sixteenth lifeboat and was given a baby to look after. Others followed her into the lifeboat. The baby was returned to its mother's arms after they were rescued.

When World War I began, Violet was selected to serve as a stewardess for the British Red Cross, and on November 21, 1916 she was on board the *HMHS Britannic,* which had been converted to a hospital ship, when it hit a mine and sank in the Aegean Sea. From the time of the explosion, the ship took only 57 minutes to completely sink. The *HMHS Britannic* was the largest ship to be lost during World War I, and thirty people died in the tragedy. As the ship went under, Violet was forced to jump off her lifeboat and was pulled under the water. She hit her head on the side of the ship, but miraculously was able to surface and be rescued. Years later, it was determined that she had suffered a concussion. Before the *Britannic* was lost, Violet made sure to grab her toothbrush because it was the one item she most missed after her *Titanic* experience.

Surely a band of angels was watching over her… and her toothbrush.

Often these amazing experiences are chalked up to being mere coincidences, but surely angels are there to help us along the way as we sometimes trip or fall on our path through life. Life is a series of learning experiences, some wonderful, and some so special, they are life-changing events.

Angels guide, protect, inspire, motivate and encourage us, depending on what we need at the time, and give us wisdom and strength when we need it. They help us find peace when we are in need of tranquility, and provide guidance and encouragement during difficult times. There are occasions when they provide a dramatic rescue in a dangerous situation.

After they read my book *When Angels Call Your Name*, a number of people have told me, "I could have been in your book, I have an angel story." Therefore, I began to entertain the idea of writing a sequel and eventually found people from all over the world who related wonderful stories of amazing events in their lives, events that left lasting impressions. I am constantly amazed at how many people have had these beautiful, sometimes life-changing experiences that are more than mere coincidences.

At an art fair in Chautauqua, New York, I met a lovely woman who had a delightful story about a butterfly that sat by her for hours as she painted silk scarves, one of which I chose to buy, not knowing it had a story that went with it.The artist had named the blue and violet scarf *Butterfly Wings*.

There are stories about a lady from Orlando who had a touching story about a puppy, a man who swallowed a "killer mint," and a mother who unknowingly saved her son's life with a long-distance phone call.

On a visit to Australia, I met a wonderful world traveler named Myra who had three beautiful stories to share with me about unusual coincidences in Turkey, Israel and England.

Read Bill's story about a fabulous dinner he was preparing for his friends, but almost didn't live to enjoy. Learn about a young man who found a dusty old chest in the attic that contained a treasure trove of valuable papers and photographs about a world-famous person. Then there is the story about a cat that decided to go to a concert. The audience found the cat as entertaining as the performer on stage.

Enjoy this collection of delightful, inspiring stories of people who were touched by an angel in so many beautiful ways. Surely there is more to life than the obvious.

1
A Farewell Dinner

Bill

It happened in the summer of 1975, when I was preparing to leave my faculty position at Washington University, St. Louis, and head to a new faculty position starting that fall in Seattle at the University of Washington. I was preparing a going away dinner for seven of my colleagues and friends as a way of saying goodbye.

However, before I get into the description of a most extraordinary event that probably saved my life, I need to back up and provide some background. St. Louis was my first home away from home after I left California. In 1964, I had gone there to get a PhD degree in the social sciences.

My mother and I were quite close, and as the unexpected second son born ten years after my brother, to a mother who was at least 43, I was mightily spoiled and close to my parents. My mother called almost every evening from San Francisco, always getting the time difference wrong, and frequently waking me. She would remind me of legal papers I needed to sign and other family chores, which having been awakened from new sleep, I would promptly forget when I woke up the next morning, much to my mother's consternation.

Scrolling forward to this day in the mid-summer of 1975, I had arranged a Julia Child menu of really hard to get ingredients, which was a challenge in my small upper-floor apartment that had the smallest kitchen I ever had: an electric stove which consisted of two large electric cooking plates, a countertop of about three feet by four feet, a sink and small refrigerator. The outside wall of the windowless kitchen was the masonry wall of the building's hallway, not quite six feet from the stove, if that. Yet, in that small kitchen, I was about to prepare a gourmet feast for my friends.

The menu was wonderful: Tornados Rossini, a wonderful stack consisting of a thin slice of toast that had been fried in ghee (a form of clarified butter that is commonly used in South Asian cuisine); on top of that a thin slice of artichoke heart; on top of that goose liver and shavings of black truffle, then the filet, and on top of that more goose liver and shaved truffle, before being finished under the broiler and drizzled with Madeira sauce. All this would be accompanied by braised endives, watercress salad, steamed white asparagus, and golden brown baby potatoes, browned in butter. To begin, there would be turtle soup with some sherry and for dessert, a magnificent Charlotte Malakoff, a wall of ladyfingers enclosing a kirsch-flavored almond cream decorated with Chantilly cream and berries.

I had to search all over St. Louis for fresh artichokes and found eight of them. In the meantime, all the rest of the menu was either still in the refrigerator or cupboards. In the middle of the afternoon, I had laid out the artichokes, trimmed and cleaned them in preparation for boiling them on the stove. I placed the artichokes in two large Pyrex bowls filled with water on the electric cooking plates, electric turned on high and I was standing in front of the stove, exasperated because the water was not coming to a boil.

At that point, my phone rang and I had to leave the kitchen, dash through the living room to the small alcove hallway that connected the bedroom with the bathroom. There were no cell phones on those days. The apartment's single phone was in that alcove, attached to the wall by a six-foot long cord. I answered it, and it was my mother who never, in all the years I was in St. Louis, had called at three o'clock in the afternoon. I was worried and asked her if she was all right, and she said yes, but she was worried about me and wondered if I was all right. It was at that very moment that there was an explosion in the kitchen!

I put the phone down, went running to the kitchen, and to my utter amazement saw that the Pyrex bowls had exploded, soaking the electric stove and spraying Pyrex glass all over the kitchen. The wall in back of where I was standing had knife-like slivers of glass embedded in it. The stove was a mess. There was a puddle of water, broken pieces of glass, and bits of artichoke all over the floor. I couldn't even walk into the kitchen for fear of electrocution and getting cut on glass.

I went back to the phone and told my mother what had happened. Her next words were, "What is the matter with you! Haven't I taught you that you never put Pyrex directly on a heat source? Throw all the exposed food out!" And she hung up.

I called building maintenance and they came up and turned the electricity off, soaked up the water on the stove and floor, and pulled out the knives of Pyrex that were embedded in the masonry wall behind the spot where I was standing just a short time earlier. They were literally white faced. They realized that they might have had to deal with a much worse scenario!

After they cleaned up the kitchen, I went back out and found eight more artichokes, had them steamed, and at six o'clock that evening my guests arrived and we had a delightful dinner.

That call saved my life, or at least saved me from terrible injury.

All my mother could say was that she just had this strong message to call me, the only afternoon call she had ever made to St. Louis.

All I can say is that I never heard Julia Child warn cooks about boiling water in Pyrex bowls!

2
The Pool Party

Marcia

I believe that angels are certainly everywhere and here is *my* angel experience.

It was a very warm August day, three days before my thirteenth birthday and my parents had invited the family of a close friend to join us for a pool party and barbecue at our house.

My five brothers and sisters and the five children of our guest family were all in and out of the pool while the adults were cooking. My father was on the deck of the pool, having taken on the important job of lifeguard. He is a redhead and always wore a hat and white zinc oxide on his nose so he wouldn't get sunburned. The kids always teased him about the white nose.

At some point in the late afternoon, I was standing on the narrow edge of the pool when suddenly I felt someone push me into the water, gently, but insistently. I couldn't believe I had been pushed into the pool, but once underwater, I could see someone lying on the bottom of the pool!

I swam as hard as I could to the bottom and it was my father, unconscious with blood coming from his nose. I grabbed him by the arms and dragged him upward and toward the ladder. He was too heavy for me to lift out of the pool and since my brothers, sisters and our friends had not noticed that anything was amiss, I wrapped my dad's arms around the ladder so he would not slip under again and quickly climbed out of the pool. I yelled for my mother and the other two adults telling them that my father was hurt and that I found him on the bottom of the pool.

My parents' friend, Bob, dragged my father out of the water, while my mother called the EMTs and ambulance. Before we knew it, the rescue squad was there and they took my father to the local hospital where he spent six weeks in the Intensive Care Unit. Thankfully, he was fine and had no permanent brain damage.

I found out later that no one was near me when I was "pushed" into the pool, so I believe in angels because an angel saved my father's life that day, and changed the fate of our whole family.

3
Does God Exist?

Brian

This story began years ago in the High School Library of LaMoure, North Dakota, a small city of less than a thousand people. About a half dozen of us, including one of the other passengers who would survive that crash, were having a discussion of whether or not God really existed. I remember saying I would need some sort of proof.

After school let out, one of the other classmates who was in on the conversation along with his younger brother and I, decided we would take my car to Oakes, North Dakota, about thirty miles southeast of LaMoure. On the way back we thought we should take the shortcut home to try to make up some time since we were running a little late and it was already dark.

The short cut consisted of gravel roads. We turned off the main highway and were heading down the gravel road when I must have fallen asleep behind the wheel because all of a sudden I remembered seeing the car sliding one way on the loose gravel. I tried to correct it by steering into the slide and we ended up sliding the other way, and down into the ditch we went! It was a very bumpy slide followed by the feeling of being flipped around. It seems that the flipping around was caused *by hitting a tree!*

I was a little dazed, but soon realized *I was upside down*! I tried to find the door handle in the dark, but only found the window hand crank. Most cars back then didn't have electric windows and if they did, I probably would not be here today. I rolled the window down and managed to crawl through it. Once I got out of the car, I saw that it was upside down and the engine compartment was slowly *burning*!

I quickly looked around and saw a light coming from a farmhouse that was only about twenty yards away. I ran to the house and banged on the door. A lady answered and I must have scared her a little since I was injured and didn't know it. My face and neck were covered in blood because my chin was split open. (Later we speculated that it hit the steering wheel on impact.) In those days we didn’t have seat belts or airbags.

I told her two other people were in the car and it was on fire, and her husband immediately headed to the burning vehicle to try to get them out. I grabbed a coffeepot thinking if I filled it with water, I could put out the fire. The faucet had to be the slowest running water I had ever seen. There was very little pressure and it felt like it took five minutes to fill a twenty-cup coffeepot. When the pot was finally full, I headed for the door, only to drop it, breaking off the spout and spilling the water all over the floor. As I looked up from my mess, I saw the car had become *completely engulfed in flames!*

My heart sank. I thought the two other passengers never made it out. However, just about that time, out of the darkness my friends appeared. One looked pretty good, but the other looked a mess; his whole face, neck and shirt were covered in blood. It turned out that he only had a small cut above his eyebrow, but as we all know, facial cuts bleed the worst.

All of us were taken back to the hospital in Oakes and observed for the night. The kid with the cut on the eyebrow got a couple of stitches. I had about fifteen stitches to close up the cut on my chin, and the other occupant was suffering with nothing more than a few aching muscles and some black and blue marks.

Three people survived a car wreck that hit a tree, flipped over, landed on its top, and burned beyond recognition. None of us were wearing a seat belt, none of us got ejected from the car, and we all walked away from it pretty much unharmed.

So in my opinion, does God exist? YES! And I give him the Glory for allowing me to entertain people all across the United States.

Brian Hoffman, Red Skelton Impersonator

Red Skelton was a famous comedian although he considered himself a clown. He created numerous characters, including Clem Kaddiddlehopper, George Appleby, a little boy, and seagulls Gertrude and Heathcliffe, and entertained audiences for several decades. In 1951, The Red Skelton Hour premiered on NBC and for the next twenty years his show consistently stayed in the top twenty, both on NBC and later on CBS.

Brian Hoffman now travels the country, dressed as Red Skelton, portraying his many characters, such as Clem Kaddiddlehopper, still delighting audiences.

4
Stopping to Smell the Roses

Marilyn

Moving day was uncomfortably close, yet there was so much to do. I was wrapping up my Real Estate career and facilitating a divorce support group once a week, while trying to pack and move clear across the country to Arizona. I had been divorced for three years and decided a chapter in my life was over, it was time to move and start fresh. I didn't want to be known as someone's ex-wife. I just wanted to be me.

What to keep, what to sell, what to give to charity and what to just plain throw out? So many decisions and so little time left. My grown children had fled the nest and were too far away and too busy to help. Nevertheless, independent organized soul that I was, I did not want to call for help. I could do it myself, or so I thought, but toward the end it became overwhelming, not to mention both physically and mentally exhausting. There were only ten days left until the moving truck would arrive.

Help came in an unexpected way. Diana, one of the women in the support group asked if she could help me pack. This was a wonderful group of fifteen women and Diana was their inspiration for staying the course and surviving the bitter battles of divorce. She had fled an abusive husband with just one suitcase and the clothes on her back, moved clear across the country to North Carolina, and joined the support group several months later. She had no money, a menial job that barely paid the rent for her small room in someone's home, and no means of transportation except a city bus, yet she never complained, always smiled, and was so encouraging to the others. She was the one who told the group about the free movies at the library, the art fair downtown, and other available free entertainment.

Her husband kept trying to get her to return to his abusive arms, but the group encouraged her to hang in there. And she did. But it was hard. At times she was ready to give up and go home to Indiana.

I arranged to meet Diana at a nearby supermarket one Saturday morning, offering to pick her up at her apartment, but independent soul that she was, she refused. She took two buses and was waiting for me when I arrived.

I rolled down the window and motioned for her to get into the car. "Hi, Diana. Ready to go to work?" Instead of getting into the car, she asked me if I had a few minutes to look at something. I told her I really couldn't spare the time. So much to do. So little time left. I was feeling really pressured and had more than my share of migraines, thanks to all the stress. Nevertheless, she succeeded in convincing me to get out of the car and follow her. With a sigh, I ambled alongside, wondering what it was I had to see.

Well, there on the side of the shopping center parking lot, was a rose garden, planted alongside the busy street. I had never noticed it in all the times I had been there. But Diana did. She led me to the long double row of rosebushes and I immediately bent down to smell a beautiful dark red one.

"No! Not that one!" she cried out. "You must start with the white ones," and she guided me to a white rose bush. It had a very mild fragrance, but with another deep breath I could discern the slightest delicate scent. My new horticultural guide then led me to the yellow roses. These had a distinctly different fragrance, slightly spicy, very nice. Then on to the pale pink ones. I remember this scent reminded me of the freshly watered atmosphere of a florist, very cool and pleasant. I wasn't able to linger very long in the pale pinks because my guide was anxious to get on to the beautiful fuchsia roses. These had the light rose fragrance that I love, the kind you think of as the scent of a rose... like rose perfume. I lingered a while and then knew where we would go next...to the ones she saved for last...the deep velvety ruby-red roses, blooming their very best to impress me. It was like the crescendo of a Beethoven symphony, strident and joyous. This was the heady scent of rose perfume.

Smiling, I turned to Diana, "Now I know why you brought me here. I had to stop and smell the roses.

It was such an empowering moment. I had been so deep into packing and moving. Suddenly I relaxed. It was as if a weight had fallen off my shoulders.

Diana had shown the divorce group how to stop and smell the roses, and by doing that, helped them to release some of the stress and tension involved in going through a divorce. Now she taught me a powerful lesson. No matter how fast-paced your life is, no matter how much stress you have, you must always take the time to stop and smell the roses.

5
A Miracle for Christopher

Kay

It was 1979 and I was working as director of a public welfare family planning/prenatal care/WIC and infant care program in Washington County, Ohio. I loved my job and felt I was making a difference in the lives of the people I served, but I had four children at home and felt I was not being the best mother and homemaker there, so I decided to quit my job and stay home with the children. My husband was happy about my decision, but I didn't want to give up my nursing career altogether, so I called Ruth, a friend of mine, who was the director of the foster care program in my county, and offered to foster any children coming into the system who needed "medical care and/or evaluation."

It was not long before I got a call requesting that we take two siblings, one with medical problems and the other for evaluation of physical delays. Of course we said yes. They would be coming to us the next day, Monday. The next day came and our five-year-old (youngest) daughter awakened with chicken pox! I called Ruth to give her the news and, of course, the children had to be placed elsewhere. Well, that Friday she called again and said that a child from our county named Christopher, was at West Virginia University Medical Center in Morgantown, West Virginia and had been there since he was life-flighted from Parkersburg, West Virginia to WVU Medical Center after birth thirteen months earlier, and had many medical problems and birth defects which necessitated a tracheostomy and colostomy.

He needed a tracheostomy due to a lack of air getting to the lungs. A tracheostomy is an opening surgically created through the neck into the trachea (windpipe) through which a breathing tube is inserted to provide an airway and to remove secretions from the lungs. Breathing is done through the tracheostomy tube rather than through the nose and mouth.

The doctors had been trying to find an adequate home for him in Morgantown area, but were unable to locate one. In the meantime, Christopher was refusing to eat and was losing weight in addition to his other problems. This problem was most likely due to "maternal deprivation" even though he had wonderful nurses who mothered him as much as possible and his doctors loved him and often carried him around on their rounds. He was the mascot for the WVU Hospital pediatric area.

However, by this time, it was imperative that he leave the hospital and be accepted into a family that would love him, nurture him and be able to adequately care for his physical needs. When Ruth notified the doctors that she had found a home for him, they were adamant that he not leave the area, but faced with the declining health of Christopher, they finally agreed to meet us. After the meeting we got a unanimous okay, as we "were not the typical foster parents," whatever that meant!

Anyway, in late August I went to the hospital for the weekend to meet Christopher and get acquainted with him, his problems, and his care. We took him home that Sunday, with all his equipment and instructions, his first time out of the hospital since the life flight from Parkersburg when he was born. He was thirteen months old and weighed thirteen pounds! His favorite "toys" were suction catheter packages and other hospital items. It only took a day to get him to eat and keep it down and we celebrated a big victory on Labor Day when he actually picked up a cracker and put it in his mouth, a big milestone! As the days rolled on, he continued to thrive.

An additional part of our "job" was to teach the birth parents, who had difficulties getting to WVU to visit him during his hospitalization, and were afraid of him and how to care for him. His care was overwhelming to them and though they would come to our house to visit him, they did not want to hold him. It became obvious fairly soon that they had not bonded with him and could not and would not be able to take care of his medical problems. Unselfishly, they saw that he was happy in our home and agreed to give him up for adoption to us. As an aside, he was an identical twin. The other twin was perfectly normal, but he and his six-year-old brother were raised by relatives living nearby, as the mother was not capable mentally or emotionally to care for them.

After many, many surgeries to correct the birth defects and frequent health crises, Christopher is thirty-eight years old now, husky, six feet tall, happily married with a precious three-year-old son. He is gainfully employed, likes his job, has very few health problems, and has a big heart for God and his fellow man.

We tried for many years to get the brothers together but without success. Finally, when the brothers were grown and able to make their own decisions he was able to get connected with them and their families. Christopher has become an example and mentor to his brothers who have emotional scars from their early family situations. What more could parents ask for! He is the most wonderful son a parent can hope for and calls us nearly everyday to say "Hi" and how much he loves us! Can't get better than that!

The reason I know it was a miracle is the fact that if Sarah had not gotten chicken pox, we would have had the other children in our house and would have been unable to take Christopher and since the hospital had been trying for months to find a home for him without success, there was fear for his life. Surely it was a miracle that we had the skills and became available to rescue him.

Saving Christopher
Our Second Miracle

When we took Christopher into our home, we had to install an intercom system because Christopher had a tracheostomy and could not make any sounds, so when he cried, there was no sound. That was heartbreaking in itself. Our bedrooms were all upstairs so we could hear only movement from him when we were downstairs.

One evening, after putting him to bed with the room humidifier running and his nebulizer on, and the other children all in bed, my husband and I were watching television. It was eleven o'clock and the news had just come on, when I got a feeling, a nudging that I needed to check on Christopher. He had been perfectly fine when I put him to bed. Nevertheless, I had that uneasy feeling. What caused it, I don't know, but I believe now it was God sending me a message.

When I got upstairs and looked at him trying to cry, blue-gray lips, hardly breathing, I immediately pulled out his tracheostomy tube and began suctioning him, but with no result. I grabbed him, ran downstairs and yelled to my husband to get the car, but instead my husband grabbed Christopher and said, "No time for a car. Let's run to the hospital!" Good move, as the hospital was only two blocks from our house and it would have taken longer to get the car out of the garage and drive to the hospital. Anyway, the bumping of Christopher on my husband's shoulder apparently loosened a deep mucous plug, which I could not get with my suctioning, enough that Christopher could breathe somewhat better.

At the hospital Emergency Room, they took him back immediately and hooked him up to oxygen and further cleared his airway! That was the all-time scariest moment in my life, even though there were others to a lesser extent revolving mostly around his airway and the very thick mucus he had, despite plenty of liquids, room humidifier, and his nebulizer.

By the way, he had had cardiopulmonary arrest in the hospital at four months of age, most likely from the same problem. If Christopher had not been in a home so close to the hospital, there is no doubt in my mind he would not be alive today. Thanks be to God!

Owen
Our Third Miracle

The third miraculous experience is about our youngest daughter, Sarah who had been trying for years to get pregnant without success. After many procedures and medication regimens, she was told she would never get pregnant for several reasons. First of all, when they were trying in-vitro fertilization (IVF), the fertility doctor told her he normally retrieved 25-30 eggs for fertilization, but she had only three and they didn't look good, but he fertilized them anyway. One took, but lived only a day after implantation.

They also had IVF with a donor egg that also didn't take. He told her she was in early menopause at age 37, that the chances of pregnancy were nil, and they should go the adoption route. They hired a consultant and waited and waited to adopt a baby. Finally, the consultant called and said that they were second in line for an infant. Being second might as well be 100th because who is going to say no? I was not happy hearing that. I wondered why the consultant even told them. Anyway, some months later, the consultant called to say there was a set of twins being born and they would most likely get them. As it turned out, after the delivery a relative decided to take them and once more Sarah was devastated. She became depressed and went to her internist and requested an antidepressant. She took the prescription to the pharmacy and had it filled, but before she began to take them, she decided to use up the remaining two pregnancy tests she had left after numerous pregnancy attempts, just to be sure. Both of them were positive, but she didn't think much about it as this had happened before and were false positives. When she went to the pharmacy, as luck would have it, the pregnancy tests were on sale (buy one, get one free) so she got a total of four tests! They all were positive. Can it be, she thought?

After so many disappointments, she was afraid to think she was pregnant. She called her internist who said that they were most likely false, but it was unusual for that many positives to be false, so she went in for blood test and sure enough, it was positive! She called the fertility doctor who said "…impossible, but come on in and we will check you out." After a vaginal ultrasound he told her, yes, she was pregnant and told her that in all his many years of practice, he had only one other like situation…some six or seven years earlier. He had difficulty believing it, but told her not to get her hopes up until after three months had gone by.

She was so happy, she and her husband could hardly contain themselves. They called around nine o'clock that night and asked if they might come over. We said, "Of course," not knowing why they wanted to see us. They came right over to our house to show us the ultrasound. Initially, we thought it was an ultrasound of the baby they were going to adopt, until Sarah said, "Look at the name on the ultrasound!"

"What! Oh NO! Can this be true? It's a miracle!"

The tears and hugs were abundant! Overwhelmed with happiness for them, we praised and thanked God for this miracle. I have goose bumps at this moment as I'm writing this and tears are flowing again with the memory!

An absolutely perfect and precious-in-every-way baby boy, Owen Matthew, was born September 22, 2012, and is the greatest joy to his parents and grandparents! After years of prayers by friends, family and our church, God responded with a miracle and everyone far and wide celebrated and praised God for it.

Oh, and counting back nine months from Owen's birthday, we realized he was probably conceived on Christmas Eve, the season of another miraculous birth, which is why we call him our little Christmas miracle. He is such a blessing to all and loves to sing and play the guitar. He attends our contemporary worship service with his parents, sings and actively gets into the music while his eyes are glued to his hero, the guitarist, who frequently lets him strum his guitar after the service.

Now Christopher's son and Sara's son play together, like brothers. The families moved to be near the other so the children could grow up together.

6
A Member of the Audience

Eileen

In 2006, I performed a fundraiser concert at the home of a dear friend in Patagonia, Arizona, which is south of Tucson, about halfway to the Mexican border. As for my background, I am a singer – a concert and recording artist and stage performer. The concert was part of a campaign my friend was deeply involved in, to raise funds for building a performance venue in the area. My concert, entitled *It's Amazing What a Scale Can Do*, was built around the idea of illustrating composer's various techniques of musical expression. It included selections from operas and musical comedies, as well as some jazz numbers, and ranged from the serious to comic, and secular to sacred.

The concert was performed in the living room of my friend, Gini's home, which she and her late husband had designed and built with just such events in mind. There was a raised section on one end, where her piano, harp, and other instruments were, and the rest of the room adapted nicely to a space for an audience. It was a beautiful place, the acoustics were lovely, perfect for a concert.

Gini had three pets. Two were wolves, or rather, 95% wolf and the remaining 5% German shepherd or some other breed. Not surprisingly, they lived mostly outdoors and howled beautifully at the moon when the mood struck – happily not during my concert.

She also had black cat that had a bit of white on her face and paws. Jade was a sweet cat, friendly, pleasant, and like most cats, quiet. She was always happy to get a stroking by me, as well as a gentle scratch under her chin or around her ears.

Concert day was lovely, and we had a full house. The cat was nowhere to be found. She was not much for crowds, and she had apparently figured out that there would be one, so she made herself scarce.

I opened the program with music that illustrated what a composer can do with the magic of a scale, beginning with the "Habañera" from Bizet's opera, *Carmen*, and continuing with a song by Ottorino Respighi, the famous Italian composer best known for the classical standards, the Fountains of Rome, and the Pines of Rome. I continued with one by Joseph Kosma, the Hungarian-French composer, known for writing the standard classical jazz song, *Autumn Leaves*. Having exemplified with those three pieces how something as seemingly simple and ordinary as a scale can create character and mood, I then moved on to musical imitations – music that sounds like, or creates the impression of some place, mood, person or animal.

The second piece in that set was one by the 20th century English composer Benjamin Britten, from his cantata called "Rejoice in the Lamb," a work he wrote using writings of 18th century poet Christopher Smart. The song was, and remains, the most unusual, charming, and touching sacred piece I know. It is called "For I Will Consider My Cat, Jeoffrey." Here is the text:

For I will consider my Cat Jeoffrey.

For he is the servant of the Living God, duly and daily serving him.

For at the first glance of the glory of God in the East, he worships in his Way.

For this is done by wreathing his body seven times round with elegant quickness.

For he knows that God is his Savior.

For God has blessed him in the variety of his movements.

For there is nothing sweeter than his peace when at rest.

For I am possessed of a Cat, surpassing in beauty,

From whom I take occasion to bless Almighty God.

Both the vocal and the piano parts in the piece are very imitative of a cat – the way it moves, stretches, curls around, leaps up onto and jumps gracefully down from high places, slips in and out, sleeps, and so on.

The moment I started singing about Jeoffrey the Cat, Gini's cat walked quietly into the living room, continued all the way across the floor to the other side, seemingly oblivious of the audience, and sat down where she had a good view. She watched me as I sang. She did not meow or rub up against anyone. She just sat there. It was, of course, all I could do to keep a straight face. When the song was over, she got up and quietly walked back across the living room…and out. She did not appear again.

The rest of the concert went very well, I'm happy to say, and the audience was enthusiastically responsive.

And the cat?

I didn't see her again until morning, when she came up to me for a scratch and pat. She meowed nicely, and purred. Unfortunately, I don't speak Cat language, so I guess I will never know what it was that drew her to the concert for that particular number, but I hope she was pleased. It was certainly a moment I will never forget.

7
One Foggy Night

David T.

This is the first time I have ever told anyone about this incident in my life. I never even shared it with my wife until now.

When I was a sophomore at John Carroll University in Cleveland, Ohio, I lived in a dormitory and my roommate's name was Bob Dressler. He was from Youngstown, Ohio, and I was from Canton, Ohio. Both Ohio boys.

Bob proved to be a great roommate. We got along well for two semesters and one day he invited me to visit him at his home in Youngstown. I gladly accepted his invitation.

The last Friday in May, I finished my exams and drove to Bob's home on Fifth Avenue in Youngstown. Bob's parents were good people and the visit was quite enjoyable. Bob's mother made a wonderful meal and I was delighted to have the delicious food after all the mediocre food I had to eat at school. Although they offered me wine at dinner, I did not drink any alcohol that evening knowing I had planned to drive back to school after dinner. I appreciated their kindness, but turned down their invitation to spend the night.

I left their home about ten o'clock. It was a foggy, damp night and the drive from Youngstown to Canton was about eighty miles, normally less than a two-hour drive. This was about fifty years ago and there were no interstate highways in those days, only two-lane roads.

For some reason, I have absolutely no recollection of the drive. My awareness of what happened began about 2:30 a.m. when I noticed a flashing light in the rear view mirror of my red Ford and looked at my watch to check the time. It was like I had died for four-and-a-half hours!

The patrolman got out of his car and walked over to mine. Confused, I rolled down my window and asked, “Where am I?”

“Son, you stopped in front of a dock at Berlin Reservoir. If you go any further, you will drive onto the dock and fall into the lake, car and all. I’ve been following you and your speed never exceeded 25 miles per hour until you stopped here, a couple of minutes ago. Have you been drinking?”

“No sir,” I responded, thankful I had turned down that glass of wine at dinner. “Officer, thank you for being here. You will never know how grateful I am. Thank you. Thank you.”

He seemed surprised by my thank you’s.

“How far from Youngstown am I?”

“Thirty-five miles.”

I had driven thirty-five miles in four-and-a-half hours and needed to drive another fifty miles to get home.

I had no memory as to where I had been or what I did for the four-and-a-half-hour period. It scared me!

I was given a citation for crossing the yellow line, which, supposedly was for reckless driving.

I thanked the officer once again and drove off, struggling to stay conscious.

I don’t know why he was there at that time of night, but later I picked up a hitchhiker, a young boy, hoping to have company and stay awake. I talked to him while I drove, as if nothing had happened, but was only kidding myself into believing everything was normal.

When I left the hitchhiker off, I played the car radio at full blast and yelled at myself, trying to prevent loss of consciousness.

Later, I went to court and pled no contest, and then I thanked the judge. I didn't resent my being fined. I was glad to pay it. I was just happy that the patrolman came along when he did.

I knew that a powerful force had stopped me from falling into that lake, car and all. To this day, I don't know what happened to me for that four-and-a-half hour period of time. It never happened since and I hope it never happens again.

8
One More Time

Alice

My mom, Alice Schiller, passed away twelve years ago. She always told me she would come back to "visit," and visit she did.

Not too long after my mom's passing, my son, Jay had been home from college for a visit. Jay had gotten pretty close to my mom in her last few months on earth. She was living in a nursing facility close by, and every time Jay came home, he would go up to see his Grandma, bring her something from MacDonald's, and stay and talk about his life at college and the girls he was dating. My mom loved a good story about love and dating and always looked forward to his visits. Jay was a bright spot in my mom's day.

This particular night, Jay was sound asleep in our guest room, which was the room my mom slept in when she came to visit. My room is right next to this guest room. Around three o'clock in the morning, Jay, in his boxer shorts, came running into my bedroom looking like he just saw a ghost. His face was as white as a sheet. He kept repeating over and over that he just saw Grandma. He said she was standing at the foot of his bed and then she walked away.

I told him he must have been dreaming. However, the sound of him yelling woke up my other son, Joe and his wife, Sandra and they came running into my room to see what was wrong. Jay then shared his story with them. I now had three frightened "kids" on my hand, not to mention that I was *still in disbelief* at what Jay saw. I pushed it off as a dream and told him to go back to sleep, but he said he was too wide-awake to be able to sleep any more.

About forty-five minutes later, Sandra had to leave, for she worked the night shift at the time, so we all walked her to the front door. She was too afraid to go out by herself, thinking about the Grandma story. The three of us waved goodbye and then I turned around to find Jay was standing right behind me, waiting to ask me another question about my mom.

"Mom, does Grandma have a housecoat with a *very big* flower on the side pocket?"

I replied, "*Oh my God... Yes!*" I was the one who bought my mother her clothes. My son, Jay, being that he lived away at college, had absolutely *no* idea what kind of clothes I bought for her. He described to a tee the exact housecoat I had bought my mother for her last Mother's Day gift.

It was then time to go back to bed and my two sons, who were in their twenties, did not want to go to bed alone. They were too afraid that Grandma might come to visit again. Therefore we all slept in the same bed until I could sneak out and go back to my own room.

I really feel that my mom came back to visit my son, Jay, so she could say goodbye to him. Jay was the only one in our immediate family who did not get a chance to say a final goodbye to her before she died.

By the way, my mom did come back one more time to visit... just me. I knew it was her. I felt something odd, like a very cold chill run through my body very early one morning. I know it was her saying goodbye and letting me know she was all right.

I really love knowing that my mom did reach out to us one more time.

9
The Treasure Chest

Nova

Being an artist, I have always had a wonderful imagination. When I was a young man, I used to imagine how it would feel to find a treasure chest. Sometimes I imagined myself finding the famous Lost Dutchman Mine that was supposed to be in the Superstition Mountains near Phoenix, but most of the time I pictured finding a treasure chest. I loved reading different treasure stories from Arizona's pioneering days. Since 1892, thousands of people have searched in vain for the gold mine and its hidden treasure. However, I never expected to find my own treasure chest waiting for me in a dusty garage, where it had been sitting for years.

In 1997, I had to make one of the most important decisions of my life. Should I stay in school at Northern Arizona University, or drop out and step into the family business? I had to make this choice because my father was deathly ill. His doctor found that he had an arterial sepal defect in his heart, and apparently it had been there since birth. Since he could no longer work full time, I had to drop out of school and start working beside him, becoming his business partner. It was a small business, but it provided enough income for the two of us. My parents were divorced and it was up to me to look after my father.

This choice eventually led me to my father's garage. Shortly after I joined my father as his partner, I decided to clean out all the stuff that had accumulated in the garage over the years. There, inside the cracked and weathered exterior of an old steamer trunk, was the treasure I had always dreamed of. It was not filled with gold, but rather, with a missing collection of information about the construction of the famous airplane, the *Spirit of St. Louis*, which Charles Lindberg flew across the Atlantic to France.

That famous plane was the custom-built, single engine, single-seat plane that was flown solo by Charles Lindbergh on May 20–21, 1927 on the first non-stop flight from New York to Paris, for which Lindbergh won a $25,000 prize. This prize, which was an enormous sum in those days, was offered to the first aviator to fly non-stop from New York City to Paris or vice-versa. Up until that time, everyone who attempted to cross the Atlantic by air were either lost at sea or died crashing on the runway.

It was crucial that the airplane be designed to endure an Atlantic crossing. My grandfather, Donald Hall was the engineer who designed this aircraft for Lindbergh, and the trunk that I discovered in my father's garage was filled with a great treasure - papers which described in detail the construction of the Spirit of St. Louis, and more than one hundred photographs and films that had never been seen before, along with personal correspondence with Charles Lindbergh.

His job was to build a plane *in sixty days* that would be able to cross the Atlantic. He knew the tragic result if the fuel line busted, if icing weighed down the plane, if a major navigational error occurred, or if pilot fatigue overwhelmed Lindbergh.

Donald Hall became my personal hero, and provided me with a purpose springing from my family's lineage and legacy.

As the years progressed, I undertook the project of telling the story of the designing and construction of my grandfather's project: the Spirit of St. Louis. In order to do this, I went back to school, to Arizona State University and studied engineering. I have used my discovery to create *Flying Over Time: The Spirit of St. Louis Exhibition* with the help of the university and it was shown on its campus in October 2011.

My life has not been the same since, and in the process, the discovery of this treasure chest has inspired me to believe in forces far greater than our understanding.

10
"2-5-8"

Tom

About fifteen years ago, I met a man named Morris who lived in my hometown of Rutland, Vermont. His real name was Maurice, but everyone called him Morris. Although our age difference was about thirty years, Morris being the older of the two of us, we had a lot in common. He was one of my best friends in the world. He was bright, honest, always cheerful, and the best friend a man could have. He was a longtime Rutland resident and in later years, a resident of Florida. He died at the ripe old age of 85 of cancer, but up to the very end, went to every sporting event he could find. An avid sports fan, Maurice loved attending local high school basketball and football games, along with pro sporting events, both in Vermont and later in Florida. Playing poker with his friends was very special to him, along with going to the horse races. He was an excellent handicapper of thoroughbreds.

When Morris retired to Florida he was unable to travel back and forth to his beloved Rutland, but I used to visit him every once in a while. He did, however, return for his 65th high school class reunion and we got together that weekend. I didn't know it, but it would be the last time I saw him.

Morris loved sports and so did I. The biggest thing we had in common was horse racing. We both enjoyed trying to handicap the horses, but that doesn't always work, as you can well imagine. Sometimes we had favorite numbers. Mine was always 3-4-7 and

Morris's was 2-5-8. For some reason we came up with that series of numbers, but I don't know why.

Morris passed away in December of 2012. Every time after that, whenever I would go to the track or a casino, I would ask him for a little outside help.

The first time came when I was playing roulette. I was down a couple of hundred dollars. My daughter's favorite number is 16. I looked up to the sky and said, "Morris, a little help, please." Sixteen came in and I collected $800.

Morris's birthday was on May 21st and I went to the gravesite to visit him. A friend of mine had given me two scratch tickets for luck because she knew it was Morris's birthday. Thinking about Morris and all the good times we shared, I looked up and said, "I want to make sure you have completed your journey to heaven. Please give me a sign sometime if you can." Then, standing there at his grave, I scratched the tickets to see if I had won. *No luck this time,* I thought, but then I looked at the first numbers on the ticket. They were 2-5-8.

I believe Morris let me know he is safe with God in Heaven. That's good enough for me.

I will never forget my dear friend.

11
His Anniversary Gift

Pat

To Ken and Marj, each June 23rd was always a magic day. It was their wedding anniversary. Even when times were hard financially, he bought her small gifts to celebrate. She would make sure that his favorite foods were waiting for him when he came home from work on each June 23rd. Ken was tall and thin, with deep brown eyes and very outgoing. He never knew a stranger for long. Marj was petite, slightly built, with dark blue eyes, a beautiful complexion, and raven hair, which framed her face. She was quiet and reserved. Their contrasts made the bond between them stronger.

Through the years, their happiness with one another grew. They lived in a lovely home surrounded by beautiful green trees. Wildlife from the woods behind the house would creep out at night for scraps Marj kindly set out for them.

Their children were grown. Nancy, the middle daughter, was a bank vice-president. Lynda, the doctor's wife, was more than just a housewife. She surrounded her family with a lovely home and beautiful gardens, which she loved to tend. Their son, Kenny was an executive in the oil business, Peggy, the youngest daughter was married to an entrepreneur, and their daughter, Pat stayed in their community to practice law and raise her children in that beautiful town. Everyone knew each other in that small village in Ohio.

After a series of heart attacks, Ken suffered one that was exceptionally severe and his doctor suggested that the family be called in. Marj and her daughter, Pat were at his bedside for over thirty-six hours. His other two daughters flew in from California and New Orleans. The youngest sister, Peggy, was on a tour of China and couldn't be reached. Ken and Marj's only surviving son was based in London. He was trying to get home in time to see his dad. Everyone was exhausted and worried.

At 8:00 p.m. on June 22nd, Pat was about to leave Ken's hospital room. She badly needed a few hours of sleep. The doctor had assured the family that Ken was stable now and resting comfortably. He seemed stronger than when he first was admitted to the hospital. Before Pat left, he said, "Tomorrow is Marj's and my anniversary. I want her to have a dozen red roses from me."

"I'll order them tomorrow, Dad. She will love them," said Pat, kissing him lightly on the cheek. She then left, intending to return in a few hours.

A little before 9:00 p.m. Ken's doctor called. Ken had passed away.

The three sisters decided not to tell their mother, that her husband was gone. They felt she was distressed and exhausted and needed a night's sleep before facing the terrible news she would hear the next morning.

Marj was always an early riser. At 6:00 a.m. she came downstairs to start breakfast for everyone, not yet knowing that Ken had passed away. When she stepped into the living room, she cried out "Girls! Come quickly and look what's on the coffee table! A dozen roses! It's our anniversary and Ken must have had them delivered. How lovely they are! But they are fading away. I don't understand!"

When her three daughters joined Marj downstairs, there were no roses. Yet, she had *clearly* seen them. Ken had stopped on his journey long enough to leave a last anniversary gift to his beloved wife.

12
Jesse

Christine's Story

On New Year's Day, 1980, I went into labor with my second child. The labor was a difficult one because my baby had not dropped into position to be born. He was turned sideways and had to be manipulated around to be delivered. After twenty-three hours of painful maneuvering by the nurses, on January 2nd, the doctor arrived and delivered my son who was blue and not crying when he came into the word.

The nurses took him away immediately and I was terrified. I could see them working on him, giving him oxygen. I must have been making too much of a fuss because they took me out of the room. It was a while before they brought Jesse to me. They said he was okay and he was. He was perfect. Eight pounds two ounces, 22 1/2 inches long, a big baby with a sprinkling of red hair on the top of his head. He was worth all the pain.

Little did I know that this was not going to be his only close call. He would have many in his life, especially in his younger years.

When Jesse was about six months old, I started to notice that when I kissed him, he left an especially salty taste on my lips. I wondered about that and then one day, probably at the doctor's office, I read a piece of literature saying if your child had a very salty taste to their skin, it could indicate Cystic Fibrosis, a very serious disease, which would cause a lot of suffering for the child and lead to an early death. I brought it to the doctor's attention and he advised me to wait until the hot, humid Indiana summer had passed and then, if I still felt his skin was salty, they would test him. Months later, it still tasted salty and he was tested. The doctor called and told me the results were positive and talked to me about what the disease would mean for us. I was hysterical and asked if there could be a mistake. The doctor said, "No, this test is extremely simple to conduct and is also extremely accurate with a slim-to-none chance of error." He advised me to calm down and prepare to learn how to care for a child with Cystic Fibrosis. He was sending me to Riley Children's Hospital in Indianapolis in a week to have Jesse examined and learn how to care for him.

I prayed for a week straight, every day, all day, that God could let me have this one. I asked my family and friends to pray, as well. One of the older ladies I went to church with in my teen years started a prayer circle at her church, and they prayed for him, too.

The next week, we arrived at Riley Children's Hospital with Jesse. He was examined from top-to-bottom, X-rayed, poked and prodded, and we were given instructions on how to do percussion hits on his back to break up the mucus that was going to form in his lungs. We had to turn him upside down on our lap, cup our hands and pound fairly hard on his back behind his lung area. He cried so hard when we did this, and I cried with him. I thought to myself that this was going to be the most difficult thing I had ever done in my life.

At the end of the long day at Riley, we met with a doctor. He told us that he had never had this happen, but that after retesting Jesse, the results came back negative. He did not have Cystic Fibrosis. He did have a spot on his lungs they could not identify and would need to reexamine in a few months and then determine if further action was needed, but definitely not Cystic Fibrosis. I had asked God to give me this one, to give me a miracle, and he did. This was mine, and maybe the once-in-a-lifetime I would get, but I would take it and be eternally thankful for it. I have never stopped telling anyone who will listen that miracles do happen.

Jesse's father and I divorced when Jesse was about seven. Gary married again and had two more children. Both children were diagnosed with Cystic Fibrosis. His daughter died recently at around the age of twenty. His son is still living, but in declining health. While this is sad for me, and nothing I would ever want to happen to anyone, it reaffirms for me that I was indeed given a miracle for I believe this is too much to be a coincidence.

Back in 1980, I would have liked to believe that Jesse might not ever have any other brushes with death or disaster, but that was not the book that was written for this child…or me. I soon learned this was a child I would have to watch every single second. He was different than my older daughter, who rarely got into any trouble and was usually right at my side at all times.

When Jesse was just a few weeks old and my daughter was three, I was visiting my mother's home. My two younger brothers were still living at home at the time. My oldest brother, who was about sixteen had a lot of guns. All were supposed to be locked up. I had laid a sleeping Jesse on my brother's bed and went in the living room to visit with my mother. My daughter, Melissa had been playing in the living room with us, but I suddenly noticed she was not in the room and got up to check. I found her standing beside my brother's bed holding a large handgun, which was pointed directly at Jesse. I grabbed the gun out of her hands, and breathed a huge sigh of relief. When my brother came home, I asked him if the gun was loaded. It was, and there was no safety engaged. I was very lucky and blessed that nothing happened that day.

Another time, Jesse was about two years old and with us berry-picking near an old abandoned railroad track near our home in Indiana. The track was about ten feet away from the berry bushes and Jesse was playing there while we picked the berries. Even though I could see Jesse from where I was, I suddenly had one of my *nudges* or instincts that I needed to walk over to him. I did, and no more than three feet in front of him, stretched across the tracks was a copperhead snake, which has a venomous bite that would likely be fatal to a small child. I snatched Jesse up and away without incident. Had I not done this, he most certainly would have tried to pick up that very colorful and pretty, but deadly snake.

When Jesse was around three, he had several incidents, one of which was when he was with his father, who was changing the oil in the car. Gary sat a partially full oil can on the windowsill on the back porch with intentions of putting it away later. Before he had a chance to put it away, Jesse found it and drank from the can. He inhaled oil into his lungs and developed chemical pneumonia. He was in the hospital for several days with a 50/50 chance of surviving, according to the doctors. Prayer again, and someone watching over him brought him through this.

Also when Jesse was about three, we went on a family trip to the Indianapolis 500 time trials. We were on the infield, which was so big you could fit the White House, all of Vatican City, the Roman Colosseum, the Rose Bowl, the Taj Mahal, Churchill Downs and Yankee Stadium into it, with room left over. Around lunchtime, my sister-in-law was watching all of the children who were sitting in their van eating lunch. I kept going back to check on Jesse. It made my sister-in-law mad because she said I didn't trust her. Finally, after I was walking back to the van once again, my sister-in-law yelled at me, "You need to stop being so overprotective! He's fine and he's right here," pointing inside the van. *But he wasn't there.* He had somehow gotten out of the van and past her. We looked around at the huge crowd. The infield was packed with people and cars and traffic lanes for people to drive to their parking spots. I was in a panic and thought for sure we had little chance of finding him, besides being worried that he could be hit by a car. Finally, we spotted a little red-haired head bobbing up and down several driving lanes away toward the middle of the infield. I ran and snatched him up, unscathed again, and felt blessed for that. After that, my family somewhat better understood my overprotectiveness.

At around six years of age, I had Jesse with me at a neighbor's house. She had two girls, aged three and seven. We were sitting poolside watching the kids play in the shallow end. She wanted me to come inside her house to look at something and of course I said I could not because of Jesse, so she had her husband come over to sit and watch the kids. I went inside with her and not five minutes later, her husband came in with Jesse in his arms, wet and coughing, but okay. Her husband had walked away and left the kids alone. Jesse had driven his Big Wheel toy into the deep end of the pool. The neighbor's seven-year-old daughter had saved his life.

When Jesse was sixteen and he got his first car, he asked me to go look at something with him. He drove me out south of town to the gravel pits. He stopped the car and we got out and walked a short distance up the road to the spot where I always said, "Someone is going to get killed here." It was an abandoned gravel pit, perhaps five feet off the edge of the road, very deep, with no barrier between it and the road. Jesse showed me tire marks going off the edge. He looked at me and said, "Mom, I made these tire marks. I was speeding and showing off to my friend, George. The car spun around and started to go off the edge. The front of my car was over the edge. I don't know how the car got back on the road, but it did. It was weird and both of us thought we were gone. I promise not to drive like this again."

Even now, as an adult, Jesse has had a few close calls. One happened just the other day. Jesse works for a cable company doing installs at homes. There was a trouble call where the customer's cable box was smoking and had burnt up. Normally, Jesse always works alone, but on this day, a trainer and a new cable person were riding along on his jobs. Jesse opened the outdoor cable box and started to reach in when the trainer yelled for him to not touch anything! One of the wires had melted. A nearby electrical company power line was not grounded and was arcing into the cable box. Everything in the box was electrified. The trainer told Jesse that had he touched the wire, he would likely have been killed. Jesse told me he absolutely would have touched it had the trainer not been there to stop him. The fact that the trainer was with him that day was very out of the ordinary.

Jesse said, "Someone is still watching out for me."

I always believed God was watching out for me and my children, especially Jesse. And I also thought my father, who died when I was a baby, was protecting me, as I had a very rough, abusive and sorrow-filled childhood with my mother. That *nudge* or instinct that I have when danger is near…I'm not sure where that comes from, but it's definitely there. And for that, I am so thankful.

13
Dorothy's Spirit

Anita

Mom's younger sister, Dorothy carefully stretched the strudel dough on a linen cloth spread atop her oval kitchen table. No one could count how many pieces of strudel Auntie Do, as we fondly called her, tenderly turned out over the years.

This table had hosted many meals at Auntie Do's house. At dinner time, her family of seven would sit comfortably around the old table, with Uncle Iz at the head, Auntie Do opposite him, close to the stove and fridge, and my cousins around the sides. When my family came for dinner, the table always accommodated us as well. Even when our "maiden aunts" visited from Chicago, Auntie Do's table made space for us all. On holidays, with at least two dozen family and friends, we would move into the living room and add a card table.

My aunt's gentle demeanor and kind face reflected the quiet strength of my grandmother Chanah. Together with her father, stepmother, three younger siblings, and four-year-old son, Chanah left Rumania to join my grandfather in the *goldeneh medina*, the golden land of America. They settled on the North Side of Minneapolis, an ethnically and religiously diverse population that included other family members who immigrated earlier. Dorothy was the fourth of Chanah's six children.

My brother and I loved going to Auntie Do's. Her warm heart, soft contagious laugh, and the inviting smells of her kitchen always welcomed us. Uncle Iz, a six-foot teddy bear, always greeted me with a warm, cuddly hug. Their kids were more like siblings to us than cousins. We would visit at least once a week and immediately upon arriving, my brother and I would make a beeline for the cookie jar, which always held luscious snacks: cookies, strudel, *kichlech* (light, egg-y, "bow tie" pastries). The strudel was a treat reserved for the grownups, who knew how much work went into making it. The refrigerator was filled with crunchy dill pickles and pickled green tomatoes, mouth-watering brisket, veal, or roasted chicken that melted into delectable morsels on our tongues. Mom would chide us for our bad manners, and Auntie Do would say, "*Ess, ess!* Eat, eat! Enjoy." Her brown eyes would sparkle as we delighted in her tasty treats.

After I left home at age nineteen and became responsible for feeding myself, I would often call Auntie Do for recipes. With baked goods, she'd say, "Mix together flour, sugar, salt, eggs. . . ."

I would sigh and ask, "Auntie Do, how *much* flour? How *much* sugar? How *many* eggs?"

"Well, look at it and see if it looks right," she'd reply. For other concoctions, like chili or soups, she'd say, "Taste it." Sometimes, though, she would actually give me complete instructions. Mom and Auntie Do's older sister, Ruthie gave me a kitchen notebook, into which I gratefully placed each of Auntie Do's recipes.

On one occasion, I called in the middle of the night, frantic. "Auntie Do! What should I do? My dough is so sticky I can't roll it!"

Never one to get ruffled, especially about kitchen calamities, she calmed me down. "Honey, just put some wax paper on top of the dough, then put it in the refrigerator overnight." Her sage advice never failed to solve my culinary problems.

Dorothy died at age 84 in April 2000. To this day, she is Mom's only sibling whose presence I could still sense. After Dorothy's death, until Mom passed away ten years later, I knew Dorothy was still among us. Her continuing presence, though, was perceived differently by Mom and me.

I was delighted to have her on-going help with my cooking endeavors. One year, I wanted to make her popovers for Passover and looked through my notebook for her directions. I scoured the binder page by page – once, twice, three times – without success. Unable to find her instructions, I pulled half a dozen other cookbooks from my shelves, still with no luck. I shut the notebook, put the other books away, and said, "Auntie Do! Will you please help me find this recipe?" Then I opened the notebook and in front of my eyes was the yellowed piece of steno paper on which, many years earlier, I had written each ingredient and every step for Aunty Do's Passover popovers.

Another time, I searched the Internet and found what looked like a wonderful recipe for crescent rolls. I followed the directions exactly and wound up with a batter that couldn't be kneaded. Again I asked for my aunt's help and the message came: "Add more milk and another egg." It worked. The rolls came out light, crispy, and delicious.

I was comforted to have my aunt hover near me. Not so with Mom, who slipped further and further into dementia. As the cognitive veil that hid the spirits of those who passed away gradually disintegrated, Mom was able to see and talk to her sister. Dorothy often beckoned Mom to go with her to the Other Side. Frightened, Mom would become agitated. Finally, Mom's caregiver told her, "Rozee, the next time Dorothy comes to see you, let me know. I'll kick her in the butt and tell her not to come back." And so it happened. After several years of visiting Mom, Dorothy stopped coming and we heard no more about the visitations. Four months later, at age 97, Mom gave a little wave and a fleeting smile, then closed her eyes and joined Dorothy on the Other Side.

I miss them both, but know Mom is no longer frightened to see her sister. Instead, she's telling stories and laughing with the loved ones who went before her. As for my aunt's help in the kitchen, she doesn't come around anymore. I guess she's confident she taught me enough to figure those challenges out for myself.

14
Mom's Dream

Anita

Before my Mom met my Dad, she was dating Danny Greenberg. Danny was a man of large stature, trim, not fat, a sharp dresser, and I believe he was a businessman, although I have absolutely no idea what business he was in. Sometimes he would keep their dates, other times not. Danny was definitely not the dependable type. He'd make dates but she could never be sure if he would show up. He was several years older than Mom. When Mom told him about Dad, suddenly Danny decided he couldn't live without Mom and wanted to marry her, but Mom had already fallen in love with Dad and they got married on January 11th, Danny's birthday. Of course, this ruined his entire birthday.

My parents had a rough spot early on in their marriage. Mom discovered that Dad was having an affair. He was running around with a Polish Catholic woman named Katie. His infidelity was absolutely not acceptable to my Jewish mother, and Danny graciously offered to pay for a divorce. However, mom went to Katie's mother and told her what was going on and that broke up the affair, and my parents stayed together. According to Mom, Dad was grateful she took him back because he loved his family, mom, my brother, me, and would never want to give us up. Never again did Dad jeopardize his relationship with my mom. Danny still loved her, but she loved my dad.

As a young married couple, soon with two children, they lived in a third-story apartment in Chicago and were friends with another couple, Carol and Gene Greenberg, and their two young sons.

Sadly, Gene got leukemia and died and left Carol, a young widow with two young sons. She was pretty and petite with dark hair, from what I remember. Mom, ever the matchmaker, decided to fix Carol up with Danny. It was a good match—they married and had a daughter.

The years passed and though our family moved to Minneapolis, we often returned to Chicago to visit and Mom stayed in touch with Carol. After my Dad died, Mom accepted a transfer to Kansas City. Working for the government, she accumulated lots of vacation days, so she'd come back to our home in Minneapolis, would visit me wherever I lived, or would go see her sisters in Chicago. Through the years she always stayed in touch with Carol.

Mom was not someone who believed in spirits and visions, yet, one morning, prior to a planned trip to Chicago, she had a dream. In the dream, she saw Danny get up out of bed, walk into the bathroom, call her name, then collapse on the bathroom floor. She didn't really think much about the dream until she got to my aunts' apartment in Chicago. They said, "You should call Carol. Danny died." When Mom called, her friend told her, "Danny got up out of bed, walked to the bathroom, then collapsed on the bathroom floor. He had a heart attack and died." Perhaps he wanted to say a last goodbye to Mom before he left. Perhaps he still loved her after all those years. Perhaps.

15
The Killer Mint

Nancy

Do you believe in the cliché, *when it's your time, it's your time*? I never gave it much thought until one day in December when my husband should have died, but was rescued by a miracle.

Jim was the Arizona manager of a national landscape supply company. One of his job perks was the use of a one-ton pickup. Also, he was expected to take clients to lunch in order to pump up his store's sales numbers.

After a business luncheon in Tempe, Arizona, Jim put several of those red and white striped round peppermint candies in his pocket. He was driving down Broadway Road toward his warehouse sucking one of those mints when he suddenly choked on the mint and remembered gagging. Before he had a chance to pull over, *he immediately passed out!*

Broadway Road is a main artery with three lanes of traffic in each direction, separated by a substantial median. From the far right-hand lane, his truck, which had been traveling forty miles per hour, drifted across all three lanes of traffic, jumped the median's curbs, and safely crossed all three lanes of oncoming traffic during lunchtime without hitting one car!

The truck then jumped the curb on the opposite side of the road and crossed a wide sidewalk without hitting a pedestrian. Then it then crashed through a section of chain link fencing and rolled, unobstructed, downhill into a wide open grassy field. The only object in this large water retention area that could have stopped his truck from rolling on and on was one lonely tree, and his truck crashed into it. The impact dislodged the mint in his throat, popping it onto the floor mat of his truck.

Jim started breathing again and soon regained consciousness. When he opened his eyes, he found himself looking into the anxious face of a stranger. This passerby had been in an oncoming car and was stopped at a traffic light. When he saw Jim's truck cross the traffic lanes and hit the tree, he jumped out of his car and ran down the hill. The Good Samaritan was quite shaken, but managed to call the police.

The police could not believe the truck had not harmed anybody at that busy time of day. If Jim's truck hadn't hit that one tree with enough force to dislodge the mint, I would be a widow.

Jim pointed out the culpable mint on the floor mat and insisted they give him a sobriety test. He had had no alcohol in his system, but his new company truck was totaled.

While they were waiting for the tow truck, Jim asked the police, "What's next? Don't you have to write me a ticket or something?"

The policeman's reply was a polite, "No, Sir. We don't give tickets for stupidity."

16
Flight 191

Jeanne

The year was 1979. My husband and I had been living in the Phoenix area for about two years. We were Midwest transplants and were learning to love the desert. We also were medical professionals. My husband, Bob, is a physician and I was currently the Food Service Administrator/Nutritionist for a local hospital. Both of us had demanding positions and were actively attempting to move up the career ladder.

In late May of 1979, our lives were running relatively smoothly, although I did have a "problem" employee who was challenging me in almost all aspects of my management role in the Food Service Department. Bob had been putting in long hours at the hospital and his "on call" schedule was also very taxing. Thus, we were looking forward to taking a break from our careers and celebrating our eighth wedding anniversary on May 29th. It was to be a brief, well-deserved change from our day-to-day strenuous work schedules.

We were in the middle of celebrating the Memorial Day Weekend on Sunday, May 27th when we received a long-distance phone call from my parents, who still lived in the Midwest. I thought they were calling to wish us an early *happy anniversary*, but they had a very different reason for the call.

Unfortunately, they had very alarming news: my sister, Ruthie, had told them that her husband, Gene was *missing*. He was on a business trip to Chicago and was due to come home to Los Angeles on Friday, May 25th. He was scheduled on a Continental Airlines flight, but he did not take that flight according to the airline. My sister was speculating that he flew standby and got on the American Airlines Flight 191, which *crashed* on Friday, May 25th!

I was stunned, alarmed and speechless. We had not been watching the news on TV or listening to the radio so all of this information was news to me.

Eventually we learned American Airlines Flight 191 was a regularly scheduled flight from O'Hare International Airport in Chicago to Los Angeles International Airport. It crashed moments after takeoff from Chicago. All 258 passengers and 13 crew on board were killed, along with two people on the ground.

After numerous phone calls, my mom and I coordinated a trip to arrive in Los Angeles on Tuesday, May 29th. Our special anniversary dinner was canceled, and I made arrangements in my work schedule to take vacation time. Remember, this was 1979 and there was no Internet or social media. Also there were no cell phones. Many long-distance phone calls back and forth were placed to shore up our arrival in the quickest possible time frame.

After arrival in Los Angeles, I was told to contact the America Airlines representative named Jean Bell, who was assigned to my brother-in -law's case and she now confirmed what we all suspected: Gene did fly standby and was not on the original airline manifest. We all speculated that he was anxious to get home for the Memorial Day Holiday Weekend and there was room on American Airline's Flight 191, so he took the flight.

Until the September 11th attacks in 2001, it was the deadliest air disaster in the history of the United States. Because the plane was fully fueled at takeoff, the explosion and fire on the ground was enormous. The heat from the fire was so intense that firefighters could not approach the crash for close to an hour. If you check the Internet, you can find a dramatic photo taken of the plane rolling in the air just minutes after takeoff.

As you can imagine, my mom and I were caught up in many different activities such as planning the funeral, contacting family and friends, participating in getting and identifying Gene's remains, and coping with Ruthie's anger, sorrow, and pain, to mention just a few, and we were exposed to the full brunt of all of them. One of our most important priorities was to keep her and my nephew away from any news outlet. We were quick to throw away the newspapers, never turned on the TV or radio, and warned the many visitors who came to the house, not to talk about the airline crash or give any details.

I was particularly concerned about my ten-year-old nephew, Greg, and his loss in this situation. He, too, was angry. His father was suddenly taken from him in this horrible tragedy. In particular, he was suspicious and seemed to be in denial, as he didn't believe his dad was really dead. He spoke about him "walking through the kitchen door" and surprising him. He wanted to see his body or remains, but in this case that was not going to be possible. There was really no concrete proof; there wasn't a body and we were still waiting for information as to whether they could identify any of Gene's remains.

I continued to work with Jean Bell, almost on a daily basis. American Airlines was flying immediate family members to Los Angeles for the funeral and there were many plans that needed to be made regarding the funeral arrangements. I had contacted Gene's dentist and had mailed his dental charts to help identify him. That task proved very valuable as I was notified that Gene's remains had been identified very early in the recovery process. Even his plain, gold wedding band had been recovered. Both would be sent home to Los Angeles. Gene, who was only forty-two years old, was coming home to his final resting place.

I'd like to tell you about Gene. His given name was, of course, Eugene, however he was way too informal to ever want to be called by his full name. Of all the men that my sister ever dated, Gene was by far the best. He had a great sense of humor and an outgoing personality, and was the type of person you wanted to spend time with. All those characteristics would never give you a hint to his actual profession. Gene was an IRS Auditor. His roommate, Matt was also an auditor. My sister lived in the same apartment complex where Gene and Matt lived. It was there that she met him and within a few months, they were married.

As the days went by, my schedule became more difficult and sometimes even gruesome. Too many people wanted information about Gene's death, details that I didn't want to discuss. Even Greg, who continued to be somewhat in denial about his father's death, wanted to know what seat his dad sat in when the plane crashed; another request for details that I passed on to Jean Bell.

My moods were changing and I was feeling quite stressed and somewhat depressed with the tasks that I had to accomplish, but I kept telling myself that Ruthie and Greg were depending on me.

One day, my mom and I were going to do some much-needed laundry for Ruthie and were about to change the bedding in the master bedroom. Just as we were starting to strip the bed, Ruthie walked in and started screaming. “Stop that! Don't take those sheets off! They smell like Gene,” and she burst into tears. We immediately stopped and returned the sheets.

The environment of the household was becoming more tense and strained with each passing day. Ruthie and Greg were fighting with each other. My sister was unsure as to how to help her son. Worse yet, I was unsure as to how to help my sister. I worked hard to do my best with all the funeral arrangements, but I didn't know how to help her or Greg cope with Gene’s death.

By this time, my mom and I had been in Los Angeles for about three and a half weeks when all the plans were finally in place for the actual funeral. My husband, Bob flew to Los Angeles to be with me and I crossed my fingers and said a little prayer that all would go well. At last the day arrived, and much to my pleasant surprise everything went as planned. My prayers were answered.

I was anxiously awaiting my return home. I had already scheduled an American Airlines flight home for both of us and was more than ready to return to Arizona, pour my heart out to my husband, tackle all the new and unknown challenges at work, and get back to our married life in the desert.

It was a gloomy day; a spitting, light-rain-kind-of-day in Los Angeles when Bob and I boarded the American Airlines flight to Arizona. To just describe it as overcast would not be accurate because the dark, rolling clouds and the unkind, cutting wind, accompanying the gloominess and rain, combined to make my anxious, heavy heart much worse.

When we boarded the plane, I lost all my composure. I was jittery and many tears were running down my cheeks as I walked down the aisle. As I took my seat, my emotions totally overwhelmed me. Yes, I was *finally* going home, but the uneasiness almost took my breath away. Bob didn't understand and tried to comfort and reason with me as the tears continued to flow. No amount of comforting or reason stopped my pain or anguish. Eventually, Bob felt that I was just overwhelmed from all the pressure and pain of the past few weeks and he quietly withdrew, allowing me to struggle with my emotions for the entire flight.

I returned to my chaotic routine with much pleasure. Work and all the challenges were a welcome relief. I was home and away from all the sadness, stress and depression I experienced in Los Angeles. I knew, however, that I was not completely free of all the details or loose ends that I needed to tie up, so it was no surprise when Jean Bell, my American Airlines contact, called me a few weeks later. We exchanged some brief, informal information about how we were and then she immediately got straight to the reason for her call. She had the information that my nephew, Greg, wanted about Gene's seat assignment. Before she blurted it out, I realized that I already knew. Gene was sitting in seat 7A! *I was sitting in seat 7A on our return flight to Phoenix!*

When Jean Bell actually said those numbers, it was no surprise to me. Suddenly it all made perfect sense. It became almost crystal clear. My emotions on the flight mirrored or connected to Gene. Was he really trying to communicate with me? Was he reaching out and touching my inner spirit? Could this be why I was so anxious and agitated on the flight; so breathless and emotional? Or, was this pure coincidence, pure chance?

I quietly thanked Jean Bell and returned the phone to its cradle. I literally was numb, feeling somewhat dazed and muted. Nothing like this had ever happened to me. Yes, I *somewhat* believed in paranormal activity, but this was *so* personal, so out-of-character for my life. I was always so objective in viewing data and statistics, wanting only the *facts* not the subjective, not the feelings of a person or their expressed opinions, which are not concrete. I wasn't sure how I felt about this incident. I was confused and somewhat bewildered.

Years later, as I reflect on and often ponder this incident, I wonder…

Would I have had the same emotions if I were in another seat and *not* 7A?

What if I had been in seat 9F?

Was my emotion tied to that exact seat and only that seat?

What influence did Gene have on those emotions?

Would his influence reach beyond my 7A seat?

Obviously, I'll never, never know. I cannot go back, but I can continue to wonder*...and wonder I do!!!*

17
Noelle

Mark

After growing up in Atlanta, I decided to leave the South and went to college in New York to study photography. One day in 1990, during the winter of my second year, I went out with one of my friends to shoot textures of old buildings in Soho, one of New York City's most eclectic neighborhoods. Many of the buildings had beautiful nineteenth century ornate cast iron facades and I found them fascinating. We carried a 4x5 camera mounted on a tripod and a box of film.

I remember at one point we had set up the camera in the middle of one of Soho's many cobblestone streets. My friend went off to look at something down the street while I was under a black cloth focusing on the cobblestones, which were still wet from the rain the night before. When I came out from under the cloth, there was a young woman walking toward me. Until that moment there had been no one on this street in the hour or two we had been there. Not a soul.

Nonchalantly, I said, "Hi, Noelle," and she had one of those Oh-my-God-what-are-you-doing-here moments.

Of all the millions of people living in New York, what were the chances of bumping into each other? And on an empty street in the middle of New York where no one seemed to walk.

When I left Atlanta, I decided to make a clean break from my past and never looked back, didn't stay in contact with friends back home or anyone I went to school with. They didn't know where I lived, what city, or how to contact me. Noelle had graduated a year before me and had apparently moved to New York as I did. However, I didn't know that.

So there we were, in the middle of that empty street in New York, reconnecting. At least for me, it reaffirmed my choice to start a new life far from everything and everyone I knew. After we chatted for five minutes, she left and I never saw her again.

18
Double Take

Marilyn

Every November I order two of my cousin Sara's beautiful calendars, one for myself and one for a gift. She paints an original watercolor for each month and the twelve paintings are always magnificent. She has been a watercolor artist for more than forty years and I love her vibrant colors, bright flowers and wonderful landscapes, bursting with glorious colors, rich with aqua, cobalt blue, magenta, sunny yellow, and vibrant violet. I look forward with great anticipation to buying her new calendars every year.

Last November, I went to the website of the company that sells her calendars and boxes of note cards, and proceeded to place an order for two calendars. I carefully filled out all the credit card information and then placed the order. But when I hit *Send*, something went wrong. The order didn't go through and I had to start all over again, tediously filling out my name, address and so on. Once more I hit *Send*, and once more nothing happened.

By this time, I ran out of patience, and thoroughly frustrated with the process, I decided to try again the next day. I closed my laptop, picked up my "To Do" list and handbag, and headed for the door, car keys in hand, several errands to run.

On my way out, as I walked past the living room, I noticed a package leaning against the wall next to the front door. It looked like a package that might have been left by FedEx. I figured my husband must have placed it at the front door when he went out to retrieve the mail and then forgot about it. I made a right turn, walked to the door, picked up the package, and opened it. Inside was a calendar entitled *Scenic Arizona,* which was a Christmas gift from my husband's stockbroker.

What a delightful coincidence, I thought. Imagine trying to order a calendar and there was one right at the front door!

I put the calendar on my desk and again headed out, car keys in hand. My first stop was a small electronics repair shop, to pick up my husband's electric razor. The owner greeted me with a smile, retrieved the repaired razor, and then asked, "Would you like a new calendar?" I nodded, not believing this was happening, and he handed me a lovely calendar, the same size as the other, which also had the words *Scenic Arizona* written in bold letters across the cover.

Again, I thought *what a coincidence!* What were my chances of getting two calendars in one day… especially when I tried so hard to order two calendars earlier? And what were the chances of both of them having the title *Scenic Arizona,* even though they were different calendars? And both of them were free, the same size as Sara's.

This year I ordered two Sara Steele calendars with no trouble at all, and they are absolutely beautiful. My one regret was that I didn't order the two calendars from my cousin that year. I missed seeing her beautiful watercolors.

Life is full of interesting coincidences, isn't it?

19
It's a Small World

Jody

My parents, Barbara and Stanley live in Port Elizabeth, South Africa. They worked together in the family decorating business in Port Elizabeth, but are now both retired. My mom was born in Port Elizabeth and has spent all her life there. On the other hand, my father was born in Cape Town and moved to Port Elizabeth when he was seventeen with his mother, father and younger sister in order to start the family business there.

For many years they have gone down the coast to a beautiful town called Plettenberg Bay, which is about a two and a half hour drive. They usually spend two one-week holidays there in May and August annually. They have a timeshare in the Beacon Island Hotel and meet up often with the same friends and acquaintances every year. The Beacon Island Resort at Plettenberg Bay, a world-famous landmark and one of the most popular holiday destinations in South Africa, is built on a rocky peninsula jutting into the Indian Ocean.

Plettenberg has some of the most beautiful beaches in South Africa, pristine stretches of white sand. The waters around Plettenberg are filled with stingrays, dolphins and whales and visitors can see seals basking on the warm sunny beaches. The caves of Plettenberg Bay are lined with ancient artifacts that date to the Middle Stone Age, as far back as 120,000 years ago. Plettenberg is a tourist's delight and why my parents return year after year.

One afternoon, while on vacation, my father apparently went down to the local news agency to buy a telephone card to call overseas. Those were the days before cellphones and the Internet. Apparently it was the last card on the shelf that day. Him and my mom then went to the telephone booth in order to call overseas. There was another elderly couple at the telephone booth and the wife appeared to be upset and agitated.

My father is an incredibly gregarious person and immediately said hello and started chatting with them. He asked where they were from and what they were doing in South Africa. They said they were holidaying from Sheffield, England. The English woman said she had to call home urgently and did not have a calling card, adding she was pretty upset as she was in the middle of a family crisis. With that, my father said to her, “Take my card. I can make my phone calls tomorrow.” They carried on chatting and my mom said, coincidentally, that her best friend from her childhood days growing up in Port Elizabeth now lived in Sheffield. My mom added that her friend’s name is Hillary and her husband’s name is Steve, and that they had visited Hillary and Steve in Sheffield many years ago.

The English couple looked at one another and couldn’t believe what they had just heard. They told my parents that their son had been badly hurt and had just broken his leg, and he was being cared for by Hillary and Steve in their home in Sheffield. Their children were close friends and she was desperate to call Hillary and see how he was recovering.

The English couple then called Hillary to find out how their son was getting on. They said to Hillary, “We are in Plettenberg Bay and we have someone who wants to talk to you.” My mom and dad enjoyed a lengthy conversation with their old friends.

Following this incredible coincidence, my parents and the English couple spent a large portion of their holiday together, my parents showing them around the beautiful sights of the area.

20
My Sister's Story

Myra

Myra is a lovely lady I met on a trip to Australia in February 2014. She related three wonderful stories and later sent me a fourth after I returned to Arizona. This is the first story:

I left South Africa years ago and now I am living in Sydney, Australia. However, half of my family still lives in Johannesburg.

Sometime during the 1960's, I'm not sure of the exact year, my sister Ruth, who lived in South Africa at the time, made a trip to Israel and was visiting a friend who had moved from South Africa to Netanya, Israel. Her friend had been living there for a couple of years and this was the first time Ruth was going to see her since she moved.

Ruth was staying for dinner, and she was looking forward to seeing her friend's husband whom she knew well. When he arrived home that evening, he brought a colleague from work with him. There had been a conference that week with some people from the United States, and he had met this chap at the conference. Knowing they already had a guest for dinner, her husband knew it was no problem to bring his new friend home for a meal. Besides, his wife was a wonderful cook and he wanted to show off her talents.

They were eating and having a good time when the doorbell rang. It was the neighbour next door. She apologized for interrupting, but she was in the middle of baking something, had run out of eggs and asked if she could borrow some.

The hostess said, “Of course, and come meet my friend from South Africa, and my husband has also brought a work colleague who lives in the United States.”

The neighbour looked at the chap from America and stared at him. Then she started to scream! She rolled up her sleeve to reveal a number from a concentration camp and he jumped up.

It was her brother and neither knew the other had survived!

Her brother left the next day for home as planned, but he returned a week later with his whole family and had a joyous reunion.

21
With Love from Russia

Myra

My sister does not drive in Israel so she uses the buses all the time. A number of years ago she was on a bus in Ra'anana when the bus stopped to pick up an elderly lady. As she got on the bus the lady fiddled in her little coin purse for the fare. The driver said not to worry, to sit down and find the money while he started to drive off.

After paying the fare, she started talking loudly to the person next to her saying she was from Russia and had been in Israel for almost two years and she had come because her only son had managed to leave Russia a number of years earlier and lived somewhere in Israel. But she had not been allowed out at the time he left. They had corresponded for years, but he had moved and she had lost his new address. Not only that, he had changed his name to an Israeli one, and she couldn't remember it.

"But," she added, "his name before he changed it had been… (*and she said something Russian*)."

The bus driver stopped the bus and exclaimed, "*Ima!*" (Hebrew for *Mother!*)

Well, you can imagine what happened on that bus and how the people cried and cheered.

My sister never forgot that incredibly moving moment.

22
Cosmic Coincidence

Myra

My first husband, Mathew and I were visiting Istanbul in 1973. We were warned that on arrival at the airport you would be bombarded with touts asking, *"You want taxi?" "You want guide?"* However, my uncle and aunt had been there and had a wonderful guide that they recommended to us. Nedjmi (a shortened version of a long Turkish name) met us at the airport and we arranged that he would look after us for the four or five days we were there. We were eager to see everything on both the European and Asian sides. Mathew and Nedjmi arranged a price and I remember it was UD$250.00. We had a wonderful time and the last day we wanted to go to a very special place that was not at all touristy, where the Turks would go for a big night out, dancing, maybe belly dancing, and there was good food. Matthew wanted Nedjmi to enjoy himself, too, so he said, "Nedjmi, we want you to bring your wife."

"Bring my wife?" he said, amazed.

"Yes, if we are going to such a special place, you don't need to sit and watch us. Bring your wife and have an evening out."

Well, he had never been asked before to bring his wife and he was thrilled. Anyhow, he collected us early and took us to his home where we met the family and his mother-in-law who was going to babysit their little child. Needless to say, we had a super time and the following morning he came to take us to the airport. When Mathew took out the money to pay him he wouldn't accept it, as he said no one had ever asked him to include his wife and they could never have afforded anything like that.

Mathew said we had an arrangement and it had nothing to do with the previous evening and insisted he take the money. Well, we heard from them every Christmas for about five or six years, but gradually we lost contact.

Twenty years later, in 1993 I was now living in Sydney, Mathew had died and I was in the travel business. As part of my job, I was on a cruise that ended in Istanbul. I had decided to stay on and spend two days there before flying out. Since I still had Nedjmi's card, I asked the hotel operator to try and call him. I explained it was from twenty years earlier, but still I was hopeful of finding him. No luck. I asked the concierge… also no luck. I knew an ex-South African who lived there whom I spent the day with and she tried everything, but no one could find out anything.

The following morning before leaving, I was going out to see the Pera Palace, where Agatha Christie had stayed and written some of her famous stories. The other concierge was on duty that morning and I went up to him and told him I was so disappointed that I had not been able to find this person whom I had known twenty years ago. I showed him the details and Nedjmi's card. He looked at it and asked, "What did this man do?" and I said he was a tour guide. He looked at me and to my amazement said, "I know this man!"

Of the ten million people living in Istanbul, I had found someone who knew him! I told him I would be back at the hotel at 12:30 that afternoon, and if he managed to contact him, to mention my name and tell him that I was the woman who used to live in Cape Town, that I now lived in Sydney, and if possible, I would like to see him. I told the concierge not to push it in case he didn't remember me, as it was a long time ago and he had had many clients over the years.

Anyhow, I arrived back early at about 12:00 and as I walked into the hotel, there was Nedjmi walking across the lobby to meet me.

He said, “How could I ever forget you?” It was wonderful. He took me to lunch and then to the airport and that was my real cosmic coincidence – to find *that* particular concierge on duty at *that* particular moment.

23
The Number 10 Bus

Myra

When I was visiting London, I planned to meet my cousin at the Queens Gallery to view an exhibition of the Queen's collection of Faberge. I adore Faberge and we were meeting at two o'clock.

I went in earlier as I wanted to buy a few things to bring back to Australia and in particular, some placemats at Liberty, which is a department store located on Great Marlborough Street that sells luxury goods. I bought other stuff there as well and then met my cousin at the Gallery. We had a good time, but when we came out it was raining, not hard but a steady drizzle. I needed to go to Marks & Spencer to get some underwear, which my granddaughter had asked me to bring back to Sydney for her. As one of England's leading retailers, they sell stylish, high quality, great value clothing and home products, and she wanted some special underwear that they sell. Since we live in Australia, I wanted to be sure to bring back exactly what she wanted.

Instead of walking, we decided to catch a bus and were told by the people nearby that we needed to catch a number 10 bus, which would take us to Oxford Street. We duly jumped on a number 10 bus and as it reached Oxford street, it turned left down Edgeware Road. I jumped up and asked the conductor if it didn't go up Oxford Street and he said no, we should get off and walk the two or three block to Marks & Spencer, so we did.

As the bus pulled off I realized I had left my Liberty bag on the bus. I stood there and saw it disappearing down the road. I was so upset I decided to take a taxi and follow the bus. I did look on the pole where the timetable was and saw that the bus terminal for the number 10 was at St. Mary's train station. I had never heard of St. Mary's, but tried to hail a cab. However, because of the rain, every taxi was busy. I was beside myself.

My cousin said, "Myra just claim from the insurance. The packet is gone."

I replied, "I don't want the money. I want the goods I had bought."

"Cut your losses," she responded, "and lets go to Marks & Spencer."

"No way!" I wanted that package!

Eventually, twenty minutes later, a taxi stopped. I told him my story and he said it was too late to follow the bus, he would take a short cut to St. Mary's and we might get there just before the bus. Anyhow as we arrived at the station, all we saw was number 10 buses. It was their main terminal and there must have been at least a dozen parked in a row. But two were arriving as we stopped.

We jumped out of the cab and each went onto the two buses. We asked if a parcel had been left on the bus. They said we should look around, but there was nothing. Then I went to almost every bus to ask if they found a package, but no one knew anything. I was so distraught and finally asked a conductor which was the next bus going back to the West End. He pointed to one on the other side of the terminus and we got on board. I really had tried and was so disappointed.

We sat down after asking the driver if a parcel had been left and he said he had no idea. Just as the bus was starting to pull off, the conductor came down from upstairs (they were the double story red buses) and as I looked up, he said, "What on Earth are you doing here!" and I said, "You were the conductor on the bus we took to Oxford Street!" We both recognized each other.

Then he said he had the parcel I had left on the bus and was taking it back to the lost property in the West End as that was where I most likely would look for it. I didn't know there was a lost property department where you could go, but he unlocked a cupboard under the stairs and took out my Liberty bag and handed it to me.

Of all the buses and places and people in London, that was the bus I got onto… and that was the conductor! I thought that was remarkable.

Anyhow my cousin and I got off the bus at the corner of Edgeware and Oxford Street. We crossed the street through underground tunnel, as it is a very busy intersection, and then we were on the correct side.

I said, “Well, it takes most people three minutes to cross the road, but it took us forty minutes. But we got there.”

I went on to Marks & Spencer, bought the stuff I wanted, and we went on home.

24
Angel in China

Brynne's Story

On the day that was almost my last, I woke up and saw them off to work—Brenda, a foreign languages teacher and Doug, a librarian. They both worked at an International School in Suzhou, a city known as the Venice of the East because of its many winding waterways flowing through gardens and ancient historical sites. This large city northwest of Shanghai has nearly ten million residents and is constantly in motion.

I met Brenda and Doug four years earlier in Addis Ababa, Ethiopia where I volunteered with an American medical team and stayed to provide support for some older orphans, whose bright smiles stole my heart, leading me back to this Eastern African country again and again. Brenda and Doug kindly hosted me during my twice a year visits, providing a soft place to land after long days of volunteering. Since this was our first time together since they moved to China, I was so happy to be visiting them and was looking forward to our journey together along the Silk Road.

I'd already been traveling for a week or so in China—Beijing, Xi'an, and Shanghai—and the few clothes that I carried in my small flowered suitcase were filthy due to the heat and humidity of summer so I took this last opportunity to wash them. As I sat in their small two-bedroom apartment, I felt the heaviness of disappointment as I recalled our original plans. We would not be taking the train to Lhasa—or actually going there at all. Although news is difficult to come by in China, I had heard that at least two Tibetan Monks had set themselves on fire in protest of the government and its continued mistreatment of the Tibetan people. Although Chinese television continued to promote tourism in Lhasa to locals, westerners were prevented from going there. I guess the last thing that the government wanted was a recording of what was really going on in the land of the snow leopard.

Instead of visiting the former home of the Dalai Lama, I was looking forward to our journey which would take us along the historical Silk Road, a trade network that extended over 10,000 kilometers and began during the Han Dynasty.

I looked out the window at the busy intersection seven floors below and was surprised at how wide the street was. The night before, I took a photo of it from my bedroom window—three car lanes, one bus lane and then next to that, a bicycle lane—ten lanes total from side-to-side. The intersection below was always busy, a mesmerizing dance of people, cars, buses and bicycles!

As I washed my clothes, I enjoyed the view below—people and cars moving in so many directions. I smiled at the dance. It reminded me of the old 1980's video game, Frogger...people and bicycles moving quickly across the street...confidently making their way in front of and behind a never-ending line of vehicles, motorcycles and bicycles.

I was so very happy to be in one place for three nights before living out of a small suitcase and backpack again for the next few weeks. Traveling through China on my own had been challenging. It took a lot of planning—printing names for hostels, cities and train stations in Mandarin so I could make my way through a land and language different than my own. I was relieved that Doug would be taking over the planning for our upcoming journey and I looked forward to just "enjoying the ride."

Brenda and Doug returned home early in the afternoon. The rain had taken a break and the sun was shining through the remaining clouds.

Brenda asked, "Would you like to go for a walk along the river?"

I was excited about getting out for a bit and responded with an enthusiastic "Yes!" I had struggled with making my way since my arrival in China and was happy to have someone who knew the area show me around a bit.

"Can I wear flip-flops or do I need something more substantial?" I asked Brenda, and she assured me that flip-flops would be fine. After saying goodbye to Doug, we took the elevator down to the lobby, went through the double doors of the building and walked by a colorful flower garden before reaching the large intersection that had previously caught my attention. We waited for the light to change and then began walking to the other side of the street where the path along the river began.

As we crossed the street, I noticed that there were signs counting down the time remaining for pedestrians crossing the street and for drivers waiting for the light to change. The light crossing the street in this direction was very short and as we reached the middle, we realized that we only had three more seconds to make our way across four lanes of traffic plus a bike lane before the light changed, so we began to run. I laughed as I ran awkwardly in my flip-flops, my head reaching forward, arms moving beside me like a locomotive…and then I saw it out of the corner of my eye…a bus heading full speed toward the intersection! Right toward me!

Although I tried, I couldn't seem to stop my forward momentum.

And then time slowed down and I felt as if I were swimming through water. Just as the bus approached, a hand pressed against my left shoulder causing my head to go back just an inch or so. Then time returned to normal as I felt the heat of the bus against my face and saw the shocked faces, passengers' eyes connecting with mine, as the bus sped through the now green light. The bus was the only thing in motion as we made our way across the bus and bicycle lanes to the sidewalk on the other side.

Brenda yelled at me, "Do you know how close you came? You almost died! I'm so sorry that I couldn't reach you!"

As we made our way over to the path by the river, I told her, "You did reach me…you pushed me back."

Brenda shook her head, "How could I have done that when I was so far behind you?"

I thought about it for a moment and then recalled that she was behind me and that I had felt pressure on the front of my left shoulder… the palm of a hand pressing against me… not pulling me back out of the path of the speeding bus. I was surprised at how calm I felt… no adrenaline rushing through my system… a typical response to such a frightening experience. I felt warm, comforted and safe. Brenda appeared frustrated that I seemed so calm about the incident. She told me that three people had died a couple of blocks away the week before… run over by a speeding bus.

Now I know it was not my day to die… that I must still have something important to do in my life.

The day before I left for China, I had coffee with Louisa, a former colleague and friend. Louisa was an astrologer, intuitive, bright and funny. When we were saying our goodbyes, Louisa told me I had an angel standing behind my left shoulder. She could see him clearly and thought for some reason that it might be Gabriel. She said, “Well, I guess Gabriel is going with you to China!” She winked and said, “Let’s get together when you get home.” I gave her a hug and walked away.

Two years after my return to China, I bought a home very near where Louisa used to live. I knew the moment that I walked in the door that it was my house. However, before moving in, I found there was such a mess on the floor where the washer and dryer would be, that I came over a day earlier and tried to clean it. As I scraped and wiped the floor, I noticed something metallic. It was silver…a little larger than a quarter. When I cleaned it off, I saw it had an angel on one side and the following was written on the other side:

Oh dear Gabriel, help us to be diplomatic and watch over us, as you did with Christ, give us the strength to reason and the humility to listen.

I have kept this medallion of Gabriel with me in my purse ever since. Now, anytime I hear a story of an angel, I think of how one day, on a busy street in China, a hand pushed me back just enough to move my head out of the path of a speeding bus.

25
Butterfly Wings

Gina's Two Stories

I live in upstate New York in a house which was once the home of my husband's grandparents. We took it apart and moved it to its current location, right across the street. The property has belonged to his family since the first group settled here in 1845. It is amazing to be able to live in a home surrounded by family and such beautiful land.

I like to work on my patio in back of our house, which is such a peaceful place. When I am not painting scarves, I like sewing, sandblasting designs on glass, and felting soap, a process of creating a washcloth and soap in one. During the school year, when I'm not creating, I am a teacher's aide in a Special Education class.

I used to work on scarves many years ago, and this year I found my old dyes in the closet and a few silk scarves, and once I finished splattering and painting dye, I quickly ordered more scarves and more colors. It is such a fun hobby because I can do it outside in the fresh air and nature is a true inspiration. The colors I chose may come from the sky, the flowers in the garden, something beautiful I saw that day, or sometimes I close my eyes and pick dyes that way. I am thrilled that what I have had so much fun making, brings joy to so many people.

This summer, on a beautiful afternoon, I decided to head outside to enjoy the warm sunshine and dye some silk scarves. Painting dye on silk is so much fun. This blue, that purple, splatter a little yellow, and voila, you have a "Happy Scarf." That day, I tried a new technique, folding, pressing and fan folding the silk, and then dipping it in the dye. When you unfold the silk it is always a surprise to see what the dye has created.

One scarf of different shades of blue was laid out on the grass to dry when there came a little white butterfly. It was freckled with tiny black spots and it sat happily on the scarf of blue. No matter how close I got to it, it never flew away. The little visitor kept me company all afternoon sitting on the sun-warmed blue dyed silk scarf. It didn't fly away until I finished my work for the day.

"Visitors" come in all shapes and sizes to keep us company and bring us joy. I named this scarf of blue "Butterfly Wings." Of all the scarves in my collection at the art fair, this one was the most special.

She Played to the Dragonfly

One beautiful July evening, I decided to go to a symphony concert. I always find the music to be amazing. On this evening the orchestra had a guest violinist, a beautiful young lady who wore a lovely pale pink gown. Her talent was beyond words. The notes she played filled the air with wonder. Sitting there, I could feel the different emotions of the pieces she was playing.

During one particular piece, she played notes that were higher than any I'd ever heard. To my delight, over my right shoulder there came a dragonfly, as if drawn to the stage by the high notes. The dragonfly lingered for a moment, then flew down in front of the stage, right in front of the performer. It flitted about the stage, lingering longer than just a few minutes, then joyfully flew off. The dragonfly visitor had come to hear the enchanted music...maybe something it had heard before.

26
Reaching Across the Bar

Jill's Story

When I was twenty-four years old, I was bartending in a party atmosphere, wearing skimpy clothes and serving massive amounts of alcohol in a bar. I was out of school, unsure of what I was doing or where I was going, and in need of some serious advice.

One day, I found myself deep in thought…wondering… what am I doing with my life and thinking that at this age I should have at least some sort of idea of the kind of career I would like. Ten years ago I lost my mother, the most important woman in my life, and I wished she were here because she was so wise and could have thrown some ideas my way.

While bartending one afternoon, all these thoughts were running through my head, when I noticed a woman who was sitting across the bar from me, giving me looks that seemed to pierce right through me. Eventually this woman grabbed my full attention. As I approached her, an odd feeling came over me. She began to talk at a speed most people would not be able to understand. All I really could make from her gibberish was "I really need to talk to you."

This woman, whose name I cannot seem to remember, although she impacted my life greater than she knows, went on to tell me that she is a practicing medium and there was so much energy flowing through her, about me, that she needed to speak with me right then and there. Now I am surely not opposed to any of this. I absolutely believe those who have passed on try to reach out to you all the time and in different ways, and on this day it was very obvious that someone was trying to reach me.

I came around to the other side of the big, dark-stained wooden bar and sat next to this woman. She asked me repeatedly if this was all right and said she was sorry this was happening during my work. I assured her it was fine, as it was a slow Monday afternoon and my services were not really needed at the moment.

She took a deep breath and began. She told me she saw two figures; the one that stood out was my grandma and there was another woman with her. I told her I never met my grandma (my mother's mother) for she had passed when my mother was a teenager, and I went on to explain that my mother had passed ten years prior. She assured me those figures were my mother and grandma.

Then she began to speak for them. I am a pretty sensitive person, so my emotions started to run and I felt this tingling throughout my body and my eyes filled up with tears.

The first thing she told me was, "They both do not approve of what you are wearing and want you to know you are much better than this place."

Like I stated before, I was wearing tiny little shorts and a show-off-the-girls type of tank top. Knowing my mother, this was right on. This amazing woman continued to hit points I thought were unreal. She told me that they were saying I have so much potential, that I wasn't seeing my self-worth. Then she asked me if I write, or I use to write, which I did, especially as a teenager. Between my hormones and the terrible event of losing my mother, I had a lot of things to say.

For me, writing was how I was able to express myself. As I got older and went through some not so happy years, I would still write, but mostly letters to my mom. I have always thought writing was a kind of escape, the way I have been able to truly express how I feel.

This woman continued to speak to me, giving me chills with every point she hit, from seeing the color yellow and sunflowers, my mom's favorite flowers and color, to telling me that writing was the path I was meant to go down because I was a talented writer and needed to pursue this as my career. They said I definitely needed to go back to school.

At the end of our conversation, tears were flowing down both our cheeks. She then asked me if she could give me a hug. Now it's been over ten years since I have hugged my mother, but that hug that afternoon felt so real, like my mother was hugging me. And when I hugged her, a surge of energy just shot through my body and for just a moment, I was the most relaxed I had been in years.

I took all this very seriously and I am happy to say that I am currently enrolled in school. I am attending a creative writing course and now I am practicing writing on a daily basis. I am a communications major with only two more semesters left before I graduate.

This was a sign I would have been very stupid to not heed. I feel as though it was a very predominant message and I needed to wake up and pay attention. So this is what I am pursuing and I can honestly say I feel like I actually know where I am heading and what I should be doing.

People may call me crazy, but I know on that day my mom really touched me and no matter where I go in life, she is looking down on me, trying to guide me and help me. Even when I can't feel a thing at all, she is there, and always will be.

27
A Punch in the Gut

Cathryn

In 1993, on a beautiful Saturday morning in March, my nine-year-old son almost died. That morning, I had sent him with his oldest brother who was thirteen, to have his basketball team pictures taken at the junior high school, just over a mile and busy street away. Since I was unable to drive due to just having arthroscopic surgery on my knee, and my husband was out of town on business, I was confident my two sons, on their bikes, would be fine. Naturally, my oldest had strict orders to watch over his youngest brother.

I was hobbling around the kitchen, my knee in a full leg restrictor brace, idly wondering how the boys were faring, when I was punched in the gut by some unknown force. I immediately stopped what I was doing, and a vision appeared: My sons were on their bikes, waiting for the traffic to subside so they could cross the busy street on their way home. Coming toward them was an older model blue pickup truck and suddenly my youngest son darted off the curb and was struck and killed by the truck.

Suddenly, I couldn't breathe. I couldn't believe what I was shown. My logical mind said everything was okay and I accepted that assurance until once again an invisible fist hit me in my solar plexus. I dropped everything, ripped the brace off my leg and screamed for my eleven-year old son who was playing with his overnight friend, to get into the car, we had to save Jon. My son thought I was crazy, but must have registered the sheer panic on my face for he ran to the car. I drove like a maniac, weaving through the maze of streets in our subdivision to the one street that would take me where I knew my son lay dying. As we veered around the corner near my destination, I was shocked to see kids playing on the sidewalk and not running to the fatal scene. When I reached the spot where the street "T-boned" into the busy street, I jammed on the brakes and saw my two sons across the street on their bikes, waiting to peddle over to our side. Coming toward them was the blue pickup, and when my youngest saw me, he was ready to fly across the street to meet me. I jumped out of the car, held up both my hands and screamed at him, "STOP!"

Thank goodness he did. When the street was clear, I motioned for them both to ride to the car. The minute they were safely across, I told my youngest to get into the car and my middle son to ride his brother's bike home. I wasn't taking any chances!

My oldest son kept telling me how his brother wouldn't listen to him, and I knew in my heart if my vision had come true, he would never live with himself for allowing his brother to die. I know that if I had disregarded the "punch in the gut," I doubt I would have been able to live with myself either.

I have told others this story, and someone suggested that it wasn't intuition, or angels or guides that warned me, but that I created a possible scenario out of fear of losing one of my sons. I don't know the answer to that. I do know in my heart of hearts (and my gut) that I did the right thing.

I truly believe our angels and guides are with us and sometimes they use methods like the "punch in the gut" to get our attention for a quick response to a potentially dire situation. Since that time, I have listened to their guidance. And, for that one "punch in the gut", I am forever thankful.

28
Never Really Lost

Barbara

As I have gotten older, I seem to misplace things. I am not sure everyone does this, but I will put something away to keep it safe, and then I cannot remember where I put it.

Several years ago, I misplaced my faith, my unshakable belief that God was always with me, and no matter how hard I looked, I could not find it.

God has been a part of my life for a long time; in fact, I can tell you the exact date I knew the power of his love. It was February 22, 1942, just a short time after the bombing of Pearl Harbor, when our government shifted into high gear to supply war materials. Our family had just moved to Long Beach, CA. My father built ships, so the Navy told him to pack up and move, and we did.

My father liked to drive with his window open, and I loved to snuggle up to him from the back seat. There were no child seats or seat belts back then. It was a rainy day, the day a drunk drove his car into ours, and for many months, our lives would be torn apart.

I don't remember the crash, but I do remember being lifted out of the street by strangers who had stopped to help. My father told me later that I flew out the window of the driver's side of our car and was crushed between the two vehicles. I awoke again in the front seat of an ambulance, held in the arms of a strange man because although three ambulances came to the scene, there was no room for me in the back.

Then I was in the emergency room of a small town hospital. Care was not good. My dear mother suffered a compound fracture of her arm, and every bone in her beautiful face was broken.

Everyone was shouting and I could see a woman on the table. I needed to find my Mommy and Daddy. I tried to stay awake. I was in a giant wheelchair with a high back and a seat made of cane. I needed to get out of this chair and find my Mommy. Then I heard a doctor near the table say, “There is nothing more we can do for this woman; she’s gone, she’s dead.”

As I tried to get up, I felt a presence, a voice that told me to stay in the chair, assuring me that my Mommy was alive. Although we were both hurt very badly, she was alive.

I was four years old, dressed in a bright red coat my Mommy had made for me and I stayed in that chair. Of course, I did not know at the time that it was God talking to me, standing beside my fear, beside me, staying close until my father found me.

Soon the medical staff addressed my injuries, and then we both, my terribly hurt Mommy and I, went off to surgery. Every bone from my ribs down was broken or crushed, but they fixed me up and then put me in a body cast and hung me from the ceiling to mend.

When we were finally released after being in the hospital for nine weeks, my mother’s arm and my legs had to be re-broken and set again, this time properly. In the meantime, I had come down with Whooping Cough. I had been placed in a room in the Emergency Room that had not been properly cleaned and where a child had died of that ailment.

But, we were blessed; we both got well. The woman and her son, who were in the other car were not as fortunate. They died that day.

In later years, I have undergone nine surgeries as a direct result of that auto accident, but I have put off doing what my doctors told me I would have to do eventually, an extensive surgery to try to correct my twisted and deteriorating spine. I did not want to think about the outcome. I had convinced myself I could handle death. It was the thought of ending up paralyzed that chilled my heart and soul.

You see, I am a caregiver, but not one to accept help, and although I realize it is wrong to think like this, that is who I am. I also know that I am strong. I have survived the sudden death of my husband of forty-three years, and the loss of my second son due to complications from his type one diabetes that caused renal failure, and his passing stole the very breath from my soul.

I never shouted at my God; I never asked why. Now, as I try to remember that time, I realize more would be asked of me. He would take my second husband and my oldest son, but all that came later.

As I struggled with making a decision regarding this needed operation, I recall the feeling of being alone, left to fight for solutions as elusive as a soft caress of the evening breeze, answers not always offered to those who suffer, for that is the way of our Lord, all in good time. Although lost and afraid, I had to move forward. I had to be strong. I had to have this new surgery.

My doctor and I set a date, but it was a month off. I wanted it yesterday, I didn't want to have time to think about it and maybe change my mind. You see, for the first time since that rainy day so many years ago, I was afraid, and my fear consumed me. I prayed. I read the bible, I asked God to help me, but nothing helped. I tried to hide my fear, to move through the days as if nothing was wrong, but this anguish found its way to my very soul.

I told myself that I had to find a way to stay incredibly busy so I could hide from this fear. Our church had started a program of knitting Prayer Shawls. I decided this would be good for me and I bought yarn and started to knit. I followed the directions that asked us to pray as we knitted. As I worked each day, I talked to this shawl. I made mistakes, some I ripped out and started over, but when it came to knitting other Prayer Shawls, I was not able to get my heart into the job at hand. This shawl was special. I wondered to whom it might be given after I had finished it and taken it to the church to be blessed. I muttered along, hoping whoever did receive this shawl might not see all the mistakes I'd made. I just hoped that it would offer warmth and comfort to someone in need, even though it was not perfect, like our lives.

I had several chores to take care of before my surgery, an operation that would take over ten hours. I tried not to think about how scared I was, knowing I had no other choice. I had never faced fear like this before in my life, so I tried to pretend it did not exist.

I delivered my shawls to the church, several more in addition to this first one, and soon I was ready to move forward. On Monday, the day before my surgery, my pastor called and wanted to come and pray with me. When he walked in the front door, he carried a prayer shawl. He placed it in my lap and explained that the women of our church knitted these to give comfort and peace. I told him that I knew of the project, that I had made several shawls. In fact, I had made this one.

At first, he did not know what to say. Then he said that he would go back to the church and get another one for me. I said no, as I clutched this one to my heart. This was the one I wanted. We talked a bit, we prayed together and after he left, I knew that everything was going to be fine no matter the outcome. I had searched for weeks, for some sign that God had not left me and here it was.

I was not afraid anymore, and just as His words of love and comfort gave strength to that little girl dressed in a bright red coat so long ago, the return of this shawl opened my heart and soul, and I knew I had found what had never actually been lost, only misplaced.

At last, the day arrived for the surgery. That morning, I thought back on some of the other surgeries I had leading up to this one. First I had to have my knees replaced in 1999 and 2000. Thankfully, they are still working well. Then I had to have a plate inserted in my hand with wires to hold my fingers straight. That works, almost, and was done in 2004, and finally, in 2008, I had the strength to go through the major back surgery, after six attempts to do patch jobs that did not work for long.

I am so blessed. I heal well, and although the pain never goes away, I can walk. I have two 15 ½ inch rods in my back with about five pounds of nuts and bolts to hold everything together while I healed. I have a grand time going through airport security now.

I know that as Pastor Paul reached out among the many shawls to pick one for me, God guided his hand. God wrote our story and then gave us life, and along the way, we have been asked to travel many roads, some we might not have chosen ourselves. We have faced trials we did not want, carried burdens we did not want to carry.

However, one day we realize that the road we did not want is the one that has brought us to the place we need to be.

At times, the way we walk seems filled with fear, but when we need a hand, one is always there. When we cry out for courage, we find it, and as we wander, feeling so lost when asked to deal with our unfortunate situation, He touches our soul and helps us to know that our burdens have a way of teaching us humility, and how to be peaceful.

I may have misplaced my faith, but God never left my side. I know that my story written so long ago still reads the same as it did from the beginning, and although we do not know what the ending will be, we should take joy in the journey.

Life is a circle and as we continually move about on this earth, not much is left to chance. When this shawl came back to me the important thing I would remember was all my thoughts about hoping that it would not matter that it was not perfect. I had prayed that this shawl might offer peace and courage to someone who was afraid, someone who felt lost and had not trusted Him to take care of them… and it did.

29
When Time Stood Still

Rose

Upon returning from a day at the spa with my friend who was visiting from Canada, I was driving down Tatum Boulevard in Phoenix and came to a stop at a red light.

It was such a relaxing day. Our husbands were at home babysitting the kids and we were free to pamper ourselves. Since my husband was never one to volunteer to take care of the kids, I was thrilled to have this day off from mothering.

I was first in line at the intersection of Tatum Boulevard and Pinnacle Peak Road. However, when the light turned green, I was suddenly immobilized and for the next minute, time felt like an eternity. I stared at the green light, but wasn't sure why I didn't know what to do. I could hear my friend yell at me. "GO! What are you waiting for?" but I was more concerned as to why her voice was so faint and distant as she was yelling. She kept yelling "GO!... GO!" yet I never turned my head to look at her. Her shouts just bounced off me. I remained calm and connected to the prevalence of my heartbeat. Time seemed to stand still. There was this disconnect. I just sat there, staring at nothing.

Suddenly, a car soared past in front of me and in that split second, I quickly snapped out of my trance. I had resumed all body functions and now could clearly hear my friend yell at me. This time, as I proceeded through the green light, she started yelling that "we should be dead," that had I gone through the light the minute it had turned green, the car that had run the red light would have T-boned us!

I remained calm for the duration of the drive home, fully realizing how we narrowly missed that collision. However, as calm as I was, my friend continued in her hysteria. She packed up her belongings that night and left with her husband and kids to return home to Canada. I never heard from her again.

When I think back at that moment, I clearly remember a "presence" about me that day. It was unlike any sensation I have ever experienced. It was the feeling of a greater power taking over my thought process. As frightening as that sounds, it was just the opposite… a calming, reassuring comfort.

I yearn to thank the angel that saved my life that day.

30
Cruising Along

Marilyn

Two years ago, my husband and I were invited to enjoy Thanksgiving dinner in Wisconsin with his son and daughter-in-law. While we were there, we told them that our Scottsdale, Arizona, house would be empty during Christmas week while we were away on vacation, and suggested that they might like to escape the cold Wisconsin winter for a while and use the house while we were gone. They quickly accepted. We gave him the keys to our SUV, and while we were away, they spent some time in Phoenix and then drove to Sedona, a two-hour drive from Scottsdale. While they were in Sedona, he drove to a nearby house to visit our friends and accidentally scraped the fender of our SUV on the two decorative posts on either side of their narrow driveway as he was leaving. The left rear fender was slightly loosened. The right rear door had a large scrape on the paint.

Usually, we would have had the car repaired as soon as possible, but the damage seemed minor and several weeks passed without us doing anything about it. Instead we were busy preparing for another trip. A few weeks after we returned from Wisconsin, we were cruising along at 75 mile an hour on Highway I-17 through the heart of the Arizona desert, on our way to Sedona, when we heard a scary sound – *flippity flap, flippity flap* – like the sound of a sudden flat tire – but not quite.

Then it stopped.

Worried, I slowed down quite a bit.

Then it started again.

Then it stopped.

How could it be a flat tire and stop flapping? This is weird, I thought. And scary, too.

My husband called out "Pull over! Pull over!" Panic hit me and I quickly pulled over and found myself at the Orme Road exit, which miraculously seemed to appear in front of me. I inched slowly onto the exit ramp, then stopped the car. We both jumped out and walked around the car, inspecting the tires, my husband kicking each one. Plenty of air. They all looked good to us. *So,* I wondered, *what made that awful sound?*

Both of us zeroed in on the left rear fender. We found it had torn loose and was the culprit making the racket, slapping against the car. But, what could we do, out in the middle of the Arizona desert at an exit that was rarely used?

Then I noticed there was another car parked about thirty feet in front of us, and a woman was standing next to the open driver's door. She looked about thirty-five or forty and wore jeans and a tee shirt. I walked over to the car, introduced myself and told her about our predicament. She said she and her mother, who was in the passenger seat munching a snack, were on their way to Albuquerque. They had just stopped to rest a bit before going on and she chose this particular exit in the middle of nowhere, as a rest stop.

I asked her if she had some duct tape, rope… anything… that could help keep the fender from falling off. She searched her car and trunk and couldn't find anything that could be of help and after a short conference, suggested I call 911. Instead, I called AAA – after all, for years I had paid for their help in just such emergencies as this one. They said they could send a tow truck to take us to the nearest gas station. When I asked if they could bring some duct tape so I could attach the fender to the car, he said he would ask his supervisor, put me on hold for a little longer than I liked and finally came back saying, "No. They could only send a truck to tow the car to the nearest gas station and provide gas, if necessary." I thanked them and said I would think about it. The nearest gas station was still in the middle of the desert.

In the meantime, the woman, whose name I learned, was Barbara, continued to search her car for something which could help, and finally came up with a pair of scissors and a black plastic woven strap about two feet long and about an inch and a half wide. I wondered how she could fix a loose fender with those two things.

"You're in luck!" she bragged, telling me she knew all about cars, that her father was a mechanic and had taught all his children how to repair them. "He always claimed he had three sons, not two sons and a daughter. I am as good with cars as my brothers," she boasted. Then she walked back to our car, lay down on the ground next to the rear fender and before she did anything looked up at me and said, "We have the same tennis shoes." I looked down and saw, indeed, we were both wearing the exact same *ASICS*. Same color. Same style. Interesting coincidence, I thought.

Then she crawled under the car, feet sticking out, to see where she could attach the strap. In no time, she found a bolt, loosened it using the scissors as a tool, cut a small hole in one end of the strap, and bolted it under the fender on one end, found another bolt on the other end and fastened the strap there. Presto! The fender was essentially strapped to the car. Barbara assured us we could now drive the car without worrying about it falling off. We offered to pay her for solving our dilemma, but she refused to accept any money.

While Barbara was working on the fender problem, I was standing by the car chatting with my husband and Barbara's mother, who by this time had joined us, when a tour bus passed us as it exited the highway. On the side of the big, beautiful, brand-new white bus, in large black cursive letters, was written *Divine Travel. Yes,* I thought, *there is definitely divine intervention going on.*

Not another vehicle exited that ramp the entire time we were there, which was at least an hour. Only that bus. And in the two years since that incident, every time we pass the Orme Road exit on our way to Sedona, I always look to see if anyone is exiting the highway or if a vehicle is parked there. In all that time, I never saw anyone either parked or exiting the highway there…and we pass that exit at least twice a month.

We thanked Barbara and wished her a safe trip to Albuquerque, where she was going to her sister's house to pick up her father and bring him back to Sun City, Phoenix, where her parents lived. She had a day's drive ahead of her, yet was happy to help us before continuing on her way. Then we turned around and slowly drove five miles back to the Cordes Junction exit, where we knew there was a truck stop, hoping to find a trucker who could help and would provide a little more insurance until we arrived back in Phoenix. There was no way we were going to continue on to Sedona for another hour and drive all weekend with a jerry-rigged bumper…and then drive 125 miles back to Phoenix.

When we arrived at the gas station, we immediately found a trucker who said, "Not a problem. I can take care of that," and in no time, rigged two bungee cords under the car, which held the fender tightly in place. He guaranteed us the fender was absolutely secure.

For an hour, we crawled along the highway at what seemed like a snail's pace, straight back to the dealership service department in Scottsdale. They said they would have to replace the fender as well as repair the scraped area on the right rear door. The guys in the service department of the dealership were just amazed at Barbara's work. "That gal's a genius!" exclaimed one of them.

We drove out of the dealership in a loaner car packed with the suitcase and all the bags we were going to bring up to Sedona, but the guys at the service department were not keen on our driving 125 miles in a new loaner car which had only 867 miles on it, so we drove home and unpacked the luggage. So much for our weekend among the red rocks of Sedona.

Surely an angel was watching over us that day, because we stopped right at an exit, just where there happened to be someone parked, someone who knew all about repairing cars, and the fender had almost torn off, but remained attached until we were able to stop. If it had torn off, it could have flown directly at another car like a missile, probably smashing the windshield, and could have killed someone.

A few nights before our trip, we had seen a segment on the nightly news about debris falling off trucks and flying at drivers on highways, creating dangerous, often fatal situations. That day, we could have created one of the fatal statistics.

I believe all of us have angels watching over us. We are so grateful ours sent us Barbara and that trucker, and saved the life of the unknown person who was behind us on the highway when the fender started to flap.

It will be a long time before we loan our car to anyone.

31
Heavenly Music

Marilyn

My husband and I had just returned from a delightful weekend in Sedona, where we attended the Red Rocks Music Festival and immensely enjoyed two concerts, one Saturday night and another Sunday afternoon. The first piece on the Sunday program was Brahms magnificent Clarinet Quintet, a major work, which lasted about thirty-five minutes, a masterpiece of chamber music repertoire for clarinet. The presentation was in many ways, an homage to Mozart's classic quintet for clarinet.

According to Wikipedia, "at the time Brahms started composing his Clarinet Quintet, only a few works had been composed for this type of ensemble and even now there are not many." He had retired from composing, but in 1891, after he listened to the clarinetist Richard Mühlfeld play, Brahms was so impressed and inspired by his talent, that he composed the Clarinet Quintet and his Clarinet Trio and dedicated both of them to Mühlfeld.

I felt so fortunate to be discovering this piece for the first time; just watching and listening to the interaction among the five players was a moving experience. The following Thursday, we attended another Red Rocks Music Festival concert, this time in Phoenix.

Again I heard the Brahms Clarinet Quintet. Since the clarinetist was incredibly talented, absolutely amazing, I didn't mind hearing it again. The more I heard it, the more I watched him, the more I enjoyed it.

However, what do you think I heard on the radio as we were driving home from the Phoenix concert? When I turned on WBAQ, my favorite classical music station, they were playing the same Brahms Clarinet Quintet! Of all the music that was playing that day on hundreds of stations on satellite radio *that* was the one I found. And it entertained me the *entire* twenty-five minutes it took to drive home.

Imagine! I had never heard it before last week, and then I heard it played three times in one week! What are the chances of that happening? Life is full of wonderful coincidences.

32
A Gift from Above

Amy

In 1976, when I was twenty-three years old, I had walking pneumonia for two weeks and this resulted in a collapsed lung. I required a chest tube in order to breathe. During the chest tube insertion, I died on the table. They said I was dead for three minutes. During that time I went through a long tunnel of darkness and felt that I left my body. Most people who experience this say they went through a tunnel of light, but the one I went through was very dark. I witnessed the doctor announcing my time of death and heard everything else that was said in the room. I remember the nurse saying, "It's a shame she died so young."

Then I turned around and found myself in heaven, standing in the clouds before two angels. One was a young girl, eight years old who I sensed was my spirit guide, and the other was a baby boy who I knew was the one who keeps me laughing.

Next, I saw three relatives who had died. I recognized each of them. Before long, I found myself standing before Jesus who said, "It is not your time and you must go back." He raised his right hand and lowered it and the next thing I knew, I awakened in my physical body.

After that my life changed and, beginning in 1981, I began to have visions of future events involving my family members. At first, I was not sure what I was supposed to do with the knowledge, as it frightened me. I told them I had seen all of these events occur in my visions. Over the years there were visions of my children, good and bad spirits, a fire, a disappearance, a stabbing, and visits from the spirits of relatives who had died.

Eventually, I accepted this as a gift and over the years and I have shared this information with love. These visions have lasted for over thirty-four years.

This is an excerpt from the book *Visions from Above* by Amy Jamison.

33
A Question Answered

Erna

On May 10, 1940, the Germans marched into the Netherlands, quickly conquering the small country. They soon began arresting and deporting Jews to extermination camps. At that time, Amsterdam, the largest city, had a Jewish population of about 80,000, which represented about ten percent of the city's total population. More than 10,000 of them were foreign Jews who had found refuge in Amsterdam in the 1930s. One of them was Erna's father.

The migration of Jews to the Netherlands began as early as 1492 when Queen Isabel and Prince Ferdinand expelled them from Spain. Ferdinand was in need of money to purchase ships and supplies to seek gold and other treasures from the newly discovered land, and Isabella was a powerful queen who loved to wear beautiful jewels and lovely gowns, all very costly. She was also very religious and wanted all of Spain to be Catholic.

In 1492, the Spanish Inquisition persuaded the Catholic King and Queen to force Jews and Moors to convert to Catholicism or leave Spain. Until that time, Jews occupied many important posts in the government, both religious and political. Most Jews refused to convert to Catholicism. Therefore, by expelling the Jews (and Moors), Ferdinand was able to finance expeditions to the New World and fill his treasury with the money he confiscated from them, while Isabella could achieve her goal, as well.

Over the centuries, many Jews migrated to the Netherlands, including those from Spain, leaving all their property behind, most settling in Amsterdam where they could experience religious freedom. The Jewish community thrived and grew in the tolerant atmosphere of Amsterdam…until 1941.

On February 22, 1941, the Germans arrested several hundred Jews and deported them from Amsterdam, first to the Buchenwald concentration camp and then to the Mauthausen concentration camp. Almost all of them were murdered in Mauthausen. By January 1942, Jews were restricted to certain areas of Amsterdam. In July of that year, the Germans began deporting Jews to concentration camps in Poland, mostly Auschwitz, and they confiscated their property.

There were 80,000 Jews peacefully living in Amsterdam before World War II. By the end of the war, 10,000 Jews were left.

About ten percent of the original Amsterdam Jews went into hiding to avoid being deported. At least one-third of their hiding places were discovered and they were deported to concentration camps, where most of them died. Ann Frank was probably the most famous of them. She hid with her family in the attic of a home for years, but eventually, was discovered and hauled away to die in a concentration camp.

Erna grew up in Amsterdam, but she moved to the United States before the war began, eventually emigrating to Israel many years ago. She had been told that her father was a victim of the Holocaust, and that he died in Auschwitz. She had not seen nor heard from him since he dropped a postcard from the train as he was being taken away from Amsterdam.

Erna had heard that the Germans had transported a large number of Jews by train from Amsterdam to several different concentration camps. At the time the postcard had been mailed, the trains were transporting Jews from Amsterdam to Auschwitz, where few survived. Therefore, she assumed that was the destination of the train her father was on and decided to find out, once and for all, if he died there.

From early 1942 until late 1944 at least 1.1 million prisoners died at Auschwitz. Around ninety percent of them were Jewish.

Years later, when she was in her seventies, Erna decided to travel to Auschwitz with her daughter. When they arrived at that infamous concentration camp, they went directly to the barracks where there was a wall with a list of the names of 60,000 Dutch Jews who were murdered there. She wanted to see if her father's name was among the thousands on the list, but wondered how she could find his name among so many, especially since they were not in alphabetical order. In despair, she placed her hand on the wall and sighed as she looked at the huge list of names. When she looked below the spot where she had placed her hand, the first name she saw was that of her late father. What were the chances of that happening?

34
The Legend of the Dish

Margo

When I was just a little girl, my grandmother told me a story about something that happened many years before. She took a car trip with my grandfather from Philadelphia to Montreal in the years just after the Great Depression. They had been told about a family who had fallen on hard times and had a beautiful set of dishes with hand painted flowers they needed to sell. My grandparents fell in love with the dishes, paid the asking price and told the family they hoped better days would be ahead for them.

I thought the dishes were so lovely and I was thrilled when my grandmother promised me that when I grew up, got married and had a home of my own, she would give them to me. She kept her promise.

I married Jerry in 1976 and eighteen months later we bought our first home. My grandparents gave us a breakfront in which to display our beautiful set of dishes. We moved to Arizona in 1997, and I carefully sent the dishes in cartons marked fragile on the moving truck from Philadelphia. When Jerry and I opened the boxes, we found that most everything was intact from the long journey; only one small, square cake plate was broken in two pieces. I kept the two pieces in a plastic bag for many years.

Years later, when Jerry and I were at a wedding, we met Stephanie and Mo and in the months and years that ensued became dear, dear friends. One day, we visited them in their home in

Maryland, and during the visit I was helping Stephanie organize her china cabinet. We were arranging pieces in the cabinet when Stephanie received a phone call, and while she was on the phone, I looked up in surprise to see a plate that matched perfectly to my set of dishes.

In the china cabinet, there was only one piece in that pattern, and as if kissed by an angel, it was exactly like the plate that had been broken years before.

Stephanie gave it to me and I treasure that plate, and most important, the friendship that binds us together.

35
Why Me?

Gioia

Mary Grace was born in 1963, a beautiful baby girl. A year later, my son, Larry John was born. My husband and I were happy because now we had a daughter and a son, the perfect family.

Mary had her whole life ahead of her. She was very smart, finishing school at sixteen. However, at eighteen, when she was studying pre-med at UCLA, a man raped and killed her. Then my whole life changed. Actually, it changed the life of my whole family.

She wanted to be a doctor, to dedicate her life to helping others. Why her?

I was very angry, upset with the world and with God. "Why?" I asked over and over. "Why me? Why Mary?"

One day about three weeks after she died, I was resting in bed, crying and asking God *why*, over and over, when I heard this beautiful, wonderful voice. It was unlike any voice I had ever heard. I have never forgotten it.

"Gioia, Gioia, are you the only mother who lost a child?…I love you…always."

I could not believe what I had just heard. I knew I was alone in the house. No one else was there.

Again I heard the voice. "Gioia, Gioia…why not you? You are not the only mother who lost a child. I love you."

It did calm me down and I felt more peaceful, but it took me years to forgive that man. But, with God's help, I forgave the man who killed Mary. After that, I finally experienced inner peace. I became a better person for forgiving, not judging people. From that time on, I always saw the good in people because you just don't know what people are feeling and what they have been through in their life.

Life was not easy for me. My mother died when I was six years old. She had come to America with all her children, but my father had remained behind in Italy. It took many years for him to earn enough money and obtain the necessary papers to come to America and join his family. So I was raised by my aunts.

My father died in February 1981 and Mary died in June, just four months later. To say the least, that was a terrible year for me. My husband died in 2013. So I know what loss is like. But every loss made me a stronger, better person. It helped me to face life with a smile.

The best thing I learned is never to ask *Why me?* Instead, I say *Why not me?* Now my life is full of special people because I see the *special* in people.

Author's Note: A few months ago, my friend Jessica had invited me to a small, intimate luncheon for six women at her home to thank us for offering our friendship to her, a newcomer to our town. Next to me sat a new neighbor and her daughter and Gioia sat diagonally across from me. At one point during the luncheon, Jessica asked a very serious question: "Where was God during the Holocaust?" There was silence. No one had an answer. Then, in answer, Gioia said she wanted to tell a story and proceeded to relate the story about her daughter, Mary. At the end, we all had tears in our eyes and the lady who sat opposite me quietly said, "I lost a child, too. My son committed suicide two months ago."

Immediately, Gioia rose and embraced her and more tears flowed as four of us gathered around the two of them in a group hug.

We all realized there was more than one reason for all of us to be gathered around that dining room table that day.

36
A Chance Meeting

Scott

In 1998, I went through a divorce due to being an alcoholic and a host of other issues, including PTSD from the Gulf War. I realized I had to deal with those issues and finally faced them. I gave up alcohol. At last I was happy and pretty well-adjusted and definitely *not* looking for a girlfriend.

On November 2, 2000, I celebrated my second year of sobriety. Exactly two weeks later, this beautiful woman was standing in front of the building where she worked as a legal secretary in a law office. I was giving a customer of mine a ride to work, which I rarely do, and he happened to work in the same area as her building. As I was passing a vehicle in front of this building, I saw that the hood was up and steam was coming from the engine. I didn't know it was her vehicle as she was standing outside with two of her female coworkers. My customer insisted that I stop and help after I dropped him off. I initially resisted for various reasons, but he insisted, so I stopped after I dropped him off, and walked over to her car.

At first, she gave me a weird look and pretty much told me to kick rocks. I was suppose she thought I was Ted Bundy or something, but it was totally understandable. Here I was a complete stranger. So I pointed to my shirt embroidering and showed her that I worked at an auto repair shop that my parents owned and wasn't some weirdo. Finally, she agreed to let me take a look. She was able to drive it down to our shop so I could take a better look and give her some options. Afterwards, I gave her a ride back up to her work and we just really hit it off. Still, I wasn't pursuing anything romantic at all.

Even though she was the most beautiful girl I had ever seen, my self-esteem took a beating in my divorce and I was just being myself, not trying to impress her. So, we became friends and would go and hang out at the El Charro restaurant and listen to my friend play live music while we drank tea and ate their famous sticky buns.

Well, I guess things were happening that we weren't aware of because I took her up to my parent's house at Roosevelt Lake to spend a weekend with my family. My son was five at that time and they really hit it off. My mom calls her the Pied Piper of children. She's just a really amazing woman, all the way around. Well, one thing led to another and we shared our first kiss that weekend, December 29, 2000, to be exact. Not long after, she became my wife.

After we married, I spent twelve years in recovery, then selfishly gave it up, spent about five years being miserable, and recently got back into recovery after an incredible series of events that I have no explanation for other than the universe was working in mysterious, wonderful, amazing ways.

She is an amazing woman, like I said, and has the patience of a saint. She stayed with me as I went through all that.

If I hadn't given a customer a ride to work that day, if she hadn't been standing in front of that building, if her car hood wasn't up with steam rising from the engine, if my customer hadn't insisted that I stop, I never would have found that angel of a woman who is my wife. I'm truly the luckiest man you will ever meet.

37
As Grandpa Lay Dying

Susan

I lived in Pinesville, Ohio, but was staying with my mother and aunt at my grandfather's house in Eastlake, Ohio to support them as they cared for grandpa. He was very ill and dying from throat cancer. He wanted to die in his house, not in the hospital. That was very important to him.

On the evening before he passed away, I was sitting at the kitchen table reading my book, my mom was cooking and my Aunt Pam was eating a sandwich. I heard a sound at the front door and looked up to see who was coming into the house. Someone stood there taking off her shoes at the door.

She looked just like my Aunt Sis, the oldest daughter of my grandfather. She was tall, had on blue polyester pants, a rain slicker and I could see her purse. It was one of those old-fashioned black purses with arm straps. I even saw her face, actually only half of it, as it looked like she was leaning against the wall behind the door when she took off her shoes. I went back to reading so I never really saw her walk over to my grandpa's bed. We had placed the hospital bed in his living room at the time.

There are only two women in the whole family who are big-boned and tall, close to six feet. One is my aunt Sis and the other was my grandma. All the rest of the women are relatively small like my Aunt Pam and my mother. My aunt and mother are both 5'2" and about 110 pounds, soaking wet. I take after my mother quite a bit, red hair, five feet tall, ninety pounds.

I went back to reading my book and didn't really pay attention to what everyone else was doing and my Aunt Pam and mom were in the kitchen with me. A few minutes later, the phone rang and when my mom got off the phone I asked who she was talking to and she said, "Aunt Sis can't make it tonight." I was taken aback for a moment since I was sure I had just seen her come through the door and go to Grandpa's bedside.

When I mentioned this to my mom and aunt, they both turned white. I got up and went to check on grandpa and nobody was there. They may not have believed me at first so they asked me to describe what she had on. The person I described apparently was my grandma who had been dead for many, many years. Well they were spooked, but they did believe me. However, they proceeded to search every corner of the house, to make sure nobody else was in the house. I truly believe that my grandpa insisted on dying in his house because he was waiting for her after all those years. He passed away the next day.

I have been told many times that I have several angels watching over me from above. The first is my grandma and the second is my grandpa. I do believe my angels watch over me and I feel them with me every day.

38
Denali

Anita S.

My only sister was sent away to boarding school when she was thirteen and I was eleven. After that I didn't see much of her except during vacations and once she went away to college I don't remember seeing her very often. However, we did have a very strong psychic connection and there were numerous times when all I had to do was really concentrate on her, especially when I was meditating, and she would contact me within a very short period of time. I was a very anxious child growing up and at one point she told me she had trouble being around me because my energy was just too uncomfortable for her. That was a difficult moment for me.

In 1986, she committed suicide because of a spiritual dark night of the soul; she was experiencing some very extreme interactions with malevolent energies, and felt the only way to stop what was happening was to leave her body.

Four months before it happened, she told me that she was feeling terribly guilty about planning to do it because she felt she was failing me. She said that she was supposed to be a spiritual role model and guide for me, and she felt that she was breaking her agreement by leaving while I was still young, just twenty-eight. I was shocked that my presence in her life was important, or that she felt she was supposed to be very present in mine, given that we hadn't been very close for years.

During the year that she was suicidal, she moved from Los Angeles to Colorado without letting our parents know her new address. Months later, I found out they had hired a private detective who was unsuccessful in locating her. They hadn't told me earlier because they didn't want me to worry, but I was angry because I knew I could find her quickly. I sat down and meditated on her, and she called me within half an hour!

Another time, she arranged for my husband and I to change our minds about where to send my daughter to preschool because I was supposed to meet the woman who quickly became my best friend. That was over twenty-three years ago and we're still very close. I call her my sister.

Since then I have felt my sister's presence on many, many occasions and I am very aware that she has been instrumental in bringing certain critical events and people into my life. I never "saw" her however, until August 2013, when my husband and I were on an Inside Passage cruise for a week in Alaska. We were on an ATV ride outside Denali and had stopped on a trail to wait for others to catch up, when I saw something that looked like ectoplasm from the movies walk out of the bushes. Even though it didn't look like my sister, I instantly knew it was her because I recognized the energy.

I literally heard her say that before the end of the year someone I was very close to would die, that it would be hard for me, but that she loved me very much and would be there to help me through it. For the next four months I wondered who it would be and when it would happen. My mother? One of my children? My husband? My best friend?

The Wednesday before Christmas I got a call that my "second mom," our former housekeeper, Julia, who had helped raise me since I was a baby in 1958, had had a massive stroke that fried the left side of her brain. Julia was my "therapeutic relationship," the person from whom I felt unconditional love throughout my entire life, no matter what. We were still very close because we had been talking twice a week for years, and every time I visited my home town I would spend as much time with her as I could. The damage from the stroke was irreparable, and on Saturday her family pulled the plug.

Three weeks later, I had been scheduled to visit her, partly to take Julia out for her 89th birthday, but instead, I was at her memorial mass. I felt my sister there, surrounding me with love.

I know she will be with me all my life, always watching over me with the love she could never express while she was alive.

39
Wait for Me

Sandy

"You can't leave Florida," I said to myself. "The land of sunshine where you have been for almost thirty years!"

"Oh yes I can."

"You can't leave Florida with its vacation lifestyle where you have made such a successful career for yourself!"

"Oh yes I can."

"You can't leave Florida, the place you love where you have so many friends, and you can't take a one-way flight to Arizona where you know only two people!"

"Oh yes I can. Oh yes I can!" I said to myself over and over again.

No matter how many times I questioned my judgment, went over all the factors, examined the possibilities, and evaluated every pitfall, I always came up with the same answer. It made no difference how many scenarios I came up with or how many problems I posed, the same words came to mind.

"Oh yes I can."

And yes I did.

On January 4, 2006, I took a one-way flight from Ft. Lauderdale, Florida to Phoenix, Arizona. I landed at Sky Harbor Airport, and then, just as I had arranged, there were my cousins, Roberta and Michael, waiting for me. With hugs and kisses and what looked like sheer amazement, they welcomed me with open arms and extended their genuine hospitality. The first stop was dinner at a lovely restaurant, and then I was off to my private room in their lovely home. I stayed with them for one month until I got settled in my own condo in Scottsdale. Having lived for the past five years in Boca Raton, Florida, and having just gone through the worst hurricane season in history with twenty-six named storms, I did not look back. Arizona was wonderful. Having had to deal with an economy that was ravaged by both recession and corruption, I looked only one way, and that was forward. I could not wait to begin again.

The fresh start meant everything to me. It gave me a burst of energy that spurred me on in every direction. There were so many different places to go, all kinds of people to see, and always something interesting to do. Exciting opportunities were everywhere … and then I met Bob.

How interesting it was that he had moved to Arizona just five months before I did. How special that he had some challenges that took him from his longtime home in Connecticut to where he knew only two people, his brother and sister-in-law. How intriguing, that he had left his familiar surroundings behind and taken his one-way flight from where he lived to go all the way to Phoenix.

Now we were two people who had left trials and tribulations behind and traded them in for new possibilities and adventure. First we dated. Then just like a blink of an eye we found ourselves in a serious relationship. In time I moved into his house, and before long we got engaged and then married.

One day, after living together for about a year, I was tidying up our bedroom when all of a sudden I gasped, "Ohhhh!"

Then from all the way on the other side of the house Bob came running.

"Are you okay?" he asked.

“Oh yes, of course, I'm fine," I answered and then explained.

"About a year or so before I moved I had a dream. There was a man in my dream who looked like you. He reached out his hand to me in the dream and said, ‘Wait, please wait. I am not available yet, but I will be soon.' I was surprised and very interested, as well. I wanted to know more, and so I responded, 'Tell me, what are you like? What do you do?' Then, answering right away he said, 'I'm an…' His profession started with the letter "A" and had three syllables, but I could not make out the other two. I tried to stay asleep to hear it again, but it was too late. I sadly awoke. Who was that man? What did he say? I had to figure it out.

"It started with an "A" and had three syllables. Ohhhh, *I thought*, he must be an ar-chi-tect.

"Bob, from that moment on, I looked high and low for such a man, but it was to no avail, and in time I forgot all about that dream. But now I remember it! That man. He's *you!* You're him! You're an *accountant!* And you're my dream come true!"

40
The Man We Called Angel

Jody S.

When we arrived, it was hot and humid as only a summer day in Houston could be. My dear friend Nancy had taken me with her for a week-long girl's trip to see her friend. I had recently lost my daughter Kate in a car accident, and I was beyond heartbroken. We had flown to Houston, even though I was always fearful of flying and my fear of flying had escalated after her death. I was lost… hopeless… and Nancy had been kind enough to try to help. She thought it would help to get away for a while.

One day during our trip, we decided to go shopping at The Galleria, a lovely high-end shopping center. Nancy purchased something for her husband, and as we were in line to pay for it, we started talking to a distinguished older gentleman who was behind us in line. He said he was a businessman from Scotland. We exchanged pleasantries about our visit and then said our goodbyes.

Thinking nothing more about the encounter, the next day we drove to Kemah, a fairly unknown little town an hour away, where Nancy had heard the shops were quaint. We enjoyed meandering through the town and eventually found ourselves in a tiny gift store. Suddenly, we heard the words, "Hello girls." There he was, the distinguished older gentleman had appeared again. We were surprised to see him and talked for a moment about how funny it was to run into him again. With a glint in his eye and a charming smile, the man said to me, "See you at the airport!"

Nancy and I laughingly agreed it just might happen, and without saying goodbye, turned to look at the gifts in the store. We commented to each other on how strange it was seeing the man again so far from the Galleria, especially since a tourist might not have heard of the town. We turned to look for him again, but he was gone. We went outside as it had only been a few minutes since we had talked to him and looked up and down the street, but to no avail. The man had disappeared.

We stopped at a café and sat down bewildered. It was so surreal. Who was he, we wondered? Did he know I had recently lost Kate and I would panic at the mere thought of flying? What were the odds he would show up at the same time as we did in a small town and shop so far from the Galleria? Why did he say "See you at the airport?"

We never asked him his name, but Nancy and I, still the dearest of friends twenty years later, call him The Angel.

I've had many blessings through the years, including coming a long way through my grief. My Kate will always be with me and I now write novels about angels in her memory. I believe that angels are everywhere and that at times we are lucky to encounter them as humans even without knowing it. Thanks to The Angel, my fear of flying is gone now and each time I fly I look for him in the airport. I wish I could spot him once more… the man I will always call, The Angel.

41
A Mystical Experience

Hilda

No matter how often I teach a workshop on learning to deal with fear, I still experience fears. As we continue to uncover our fearful selves and our old, outdated beliefs and operating systems, our fears and reactions lessen. But then new fears crop up for us, fears that require us to go even deeper into ourselves, updating our beliefs, creating newer operating systems, establishing a new comfort zone and allowing us to prepare for our next set of fears, which always come up.

As long as we continue to grow, we will have fears. When we are asked to step into the unknown, our immediate reaction is fear. It is our natural instinct of fight or flight. I have discovered a more creative way to respond to the unknown. I now have the attitude of "I do not understand, and I do not have to." I am open and have faith that nothing can hurt me. My life is a perfect experience - for me. With faith, we have trust in the perfect outcome in all matters. The stronger our faith, the weaker our fears become.

I have had many experiences that have reinforced my desire to be open to the unknown. Some of these experiences I could not understand at the time. For example, two days before I was to teach a workshop, I had the following dream:

I am standing in the front lobby after church, talking to a woman about the upcoming workshop. I feel a hand tap me on my right shoulder. I turn around and face a slightly built man in a dark suit, not very tall, with a forced smile.

"I need to talk to you," he says in a quiet voice, looking at me and then down at the floor.

"What can I do for you?" I ask.

"I really need this workshop that you described this morning at the service. I heard you speak, and every word was exactly what I needed to hear. If I don't take this workshop, I am going to die. I'll make sure of it. I'm desperate and I have no money."

I tell him not to worry about the money, just come the next night and we will work something out. I woke up trembling. Was my success in teaching getting to me? I decided to dismiss the dream.

The next day was Sunday, and I attended church to give a three-minute talk on my fear workshop, which would be held the next day. I had planned my talk and rehearsed it well. The minister introduced me, and as I walked to the podium my mind went blank. I couldn't remember a thing. What was it that I had known so well just a few moments ago?

I described my workshop, but I was not saying what I had planned to say. I now know that what came out of my mouth was perfect for someone in the audience to hear. After the service I stood in the front lobby to answer questions. I was talking to a woman when I felt someone tap me on my right shoulder. I turned around and faced a slightly built man in a dark suit, not very tall, with a forced smile. "I need to talk to you," he said in a quiet voice, looking at me and then down at the floor - and you know the rest. It was the man I had seen in my dream the night before.

In 1995, I felt guided to apply to be a workshop presenter at the Native American Women's Wellness Conference, which is held annually. I wanted to call the workshop "Risking and Trusting Your Way Through Life." Although I have Yaqui Indian heritage, I was not raised with traditional native customs. I began praying for guidance. I wanted to be appropriate in my lessons and in my sharing. I wanted to love these women in the spirit of oneness. And I am sure that I desired to be accepted as one of them.

One of my fears growing up was connected to my Indian heritage. Unfortunately for me – and for those of you who understand – being Indian was considered shameful. How sad for us to have felt such an emotion! Shame is a travesty for any heritage or culture anywhere in the world. I was almost forty before I could proudly proclaim my Mexican Indian heritage. I wear it now as a badge of honor, never missing an opportunity to announce my ancestry.

My application to present the workshop was accepted. I was very excited, and yes, I was afraid. But my enthusiasm and commitment to the women were stronger than the fear and carried me through. I loved teaching that workshop, and I was asked back for the next year.

In my second year at the conference, I had a remarkable experience. I began by reading a poem by Guillaume Appollinaire:

Come to the edge of the cliff, he said.
We are afraid, they said.
Come to the edge of the cliff, he said.
We are afraid, they said.
Come to the edge of the cliff, he said.
They came, he pushed, they flew.

One hundred and fifty women were in the group. They were responsive, attentive, and totally present with each other and with me. I felt their spirits opening up to receiving everything I had prepared especially for them. I wanted to empower them as much as I felt empowered: the power of God, of light moving through all of us. The workshop was a great success, and after the presentation the participants lined up single file and asked for a hug. Some even wanted me to sign the handouts I had brought. I was honored and somewhat embarrassed, yet excited to be considered special to them.

One young woman waited in the front row where she had been sitting during the presentation. I had hugged everyone in line and the room was empty except for the woman who was still seated. I sat down beside her and asked what I could do for her. She took my hand and began her story: "I am from Canada. This is a far distance for me to come for a conference, but I felt a strong pull to be here. I knew there was something here that I needed to have."

She went on, "I am stuck in a situation and have not been able to move on. I am afraid. Today you talked a lot about fears and how it is all right to have them, but that we have to move on anyway so that we can discover ourselves. This I needed to hear. But the most important thing you said came right at the beginning.

"Several years ago I dreamt I was standing at the edge of a cliff with a woman who said to me, 'Jump, and I will be there.' Over and over I had this dream. Each time I could not jump and would wake up crying and scared. Over and over I have thought about this dream in my waking state. I had never seen the woman in my dream before. I couldn't place her face anywhere. Finally, last week in my dream, she said again, 'Jump, and I will be with you.' We jumped together from the cliff. Our fall transformed into a soft, steady flight as we both gently landed on a beautiful, white sandy beach. I turned to look at her face and until today I did not know who she was. You are that woman whom I have seen in this dream all this time. You are the one."

She had come for her validation so that she could move on in her life. And I had come for mine, to jump and know that I too will never be alone, that I am doing the work I have prepared for: to teach, to learn, to love, and to create.

I have learned to be fully present and listen without judgment to every story I am told. I know that the truth flows in everyone. Nothing is any longer unbelievable to me. Each one of us is continually given opportunities to live our lives from our essence, if we will only pay attention. Moment by moment, consciously or unconsciously, we are creating. In my most deeply centered self, I know that nothing has ever happened to me. It has happened for me. All of it has been perfect.

This is an excerpt from the book *Living on the Other Side of Fear* by Hilda Villaverde.

42
Do Not Be Afraid

Teresa

I was more than four months pregnant with my third child and second pregnancy. My first were twins. They had to be the last set of surprise twins in North America. But that's another story. I waited almost five years for my third child. Having a boy and a girl the first time seemed like more than enough when I had them, but as they grew, I felt that overwhelming urge to have another baby. Besides, maybe the pregnancy wouldn't be so awful this time. Hope is for the foolish though. The second pregnancy was just as draining as it was with the twins. I knew this would be the last pregnancy for me.

It was a Saturday morning and one of the infrequent times when I did not feel nauseous. The twins and their father were gone for the morning. The sun lit the kitchen and front room and brightened my spirit. During the rare moment of quiet and peace, I collected my thoughts. I was enjoying my alone time when I heard a voice. Anyhow it sounded like a voice. Audible. But maybe not to my ears but to my soul. I'm not sure that what I heard came from female or male. But I now know it was an angel's voice, deliberate and composed.

"Do not be afraid. Everything is going to be okay."

Somehow it didn't surprise me or frighten me to think that I was hearing a celestial voice. It seemed right that I answer.

"I'm not afraid."

Quickly I ran through my mind regarding something being wrong with the baby or losing it. Nope, I wasn't concerned with any of those things.

"Remember that I said this."

Okay, whatever, I thought. For a few days I wondered about what I had heard, but then I forgot about it.

The months passed. Similar to the twins, it was not an easy pregnancy. I had pre-eclampsia with them and with this one, too. This is a disorder of pregnancy characterized by high blood pressure and a large amount of protein in the urine and sometimes signs of damage to another organ like the kidneys. It usually occurs in the third trimester of pregnancy and worsens over time. Slowly, my blood pressure crept up and I was placed on bed rest the month before delivery. I did not hear the voice again…until…

I was a few days away from delivery. A C-section had been scheduled. I got up from my familiar couch position to go to the bathroom. I saw the water in the toilet was bright red. I was bleeding. One of the possible complications of pre-eclampsia is hemorrhaging. Such a condition can cause death to the baby and or mother, or severe brain damage from oxygen deprivation. When I had the twins my roommate in the hospital's baby was deprived of oxygen and was brain damaged. He didn't respond. His color instead of being a healthy pink was a pallid gray. I panicked. At that moment the same calm voice that I had heard months before spoke.

"This is what I meant. Don't worry."

What? This being was telling me not to worry? Was it a nut or what? This time I was surprised to hear the voice. Not that it would talk to me, but that I hadn't heard it for months and this was the moment it chose speak.

Again I answered. "I don't know about you, but I'm bleeding!" meaning, it's easy for you to say not to worry. You're an angel and may not appreciate the gravity of the situation.

"This is what I meant. Don't be afraid. Everything is going to be okay."

I didn't have time for a discussion. I let it rest at that, called the doctor and had an emergency C-section that night and a healthy baby girl. The bleeding, in this case, turned out to be nothing serious.

To this day I wonder at the voice. I haven't heard it since. If I hadn't heard it that night would I have done anything different? I still would have called the doctor and gone to the hospital. Voice or no voice I was very frightened. I'm not sure if I would have been more so if I hadn't heard the voice. Maybe the angel needed to encourage me even if I wasn't receptive. Maybe it comforted me more than I realized.

Postscript

The angel visited me over thirty years ago. My precious daughter is now grown. She and her husband tried for five years to have a child and accepted the reality that it would never happen. As her mom, I asked God for a baby for them. I prayed. For months I prayed. Finally, I began to feel restless. I don't know how to describe it. It was like a pressure or a burden. I asked God what it was he wanted to tell me.

In a voice so solid and with no reservation my soul was stirred again, I heard *"Your daughter is going to have a baby."*

Again I found myself talking to a voice. This time I was more reverent because I do believe I was privileged and blessed to be speaking with God.

"I know, God. I have prayed for it in faith and I know You will answer."

There was no question in my mind.

"No. It is done."

When God says something is done, it's done. I felt the peace that passes all understanding. My soul rejoiced.

In less than a month, my daughter and her husband called to announce their pregnancy. Their son Joshua was born eight months later. He is our miracle.

43
Flying High

Brenda

In the early 1940s Frances Arnold of Townville, Pennsylvania, came to stay and work for the summer at Chautauqua Institution in Mayville, New York. There, she met a young local man from nearby Mayville, Harold Freay, and they fell in love. They wanted to plan a future together but the world was at war and Harold knew that he, like thousands of other young American men, would soon be drafted. So in December of 1942, he enlisted in the army and almost immediately went into the Army Air Force. He was trained as a Master Engineer and assigned to a B-24 Liberator bomber. He soon learned when the plane was in combat he would serve as an aerial gunner. He had attained the rank of Staff Sergeant. One day, he was given a short furlough, went home and married Fran in November of 1943. Shortly afterwards he left for Europe.

The attrition rate for air crews was very high and on April 12, 1943, Harold's bomber failed to return from a mission over Vienna, Austria. It wouldn't be until May 8th that Fran, now living and working in Washington, D.C., would be notified by the war department that her husband was missing in action. Fran was sure the man she loved, the man she had married just three years before, was dead.

At that time, Fran was working for the FBI in Washington. At work one day, just by chance, she happened to see a telegram that was sent that said a man saw a picture of an airman, Harold

Freay, being taken away by the Germans as a prisoner and he was certain that Harold was still alive. Fran's spirits soared!

Sometime later, Fran received correspondence from two wounded airmen who were recovering in hospital in Italy. They related that they had been on the mission in which Harold's plane had gone down. They told her the plane was hit by "flack" or anti-aircraft fire, but that the hit had been on a part of the plane that Harold wouldn't normally have been in during flight. They told of seeing airmen parachute from the stricken craft and they felt he had a fair chance of having made it out of the stricken craft, and was perhaps a prisoner of war. This, at least, was hope, but not much. It was later determined that of the twelve crewmen in the B-24, six parachuted and were probably taken into captivity. Also, around this time Harold's picture appeared in a paper somewhere in Europe, perhaps London, depicting him as a prisoner of war. Someone just happened to recognize him and in turn, notified his mother that he was alive.

Sometime later, the International Red Cross notified Fran that her husband, Staff Sergeant Harold Freay, was indeed a prisoner of war and was being held in Stalag 17B near Krems, Austria along with about 4,000 other captured airmen. He would spend the next thirteen months in captivity. Harold would relate after the war of the constant hunger the prisoners faced. "Hungry. Always hungry. You went to bed hungry. You woke up hungry." As the war neared its end, they received starvation rations and finally, there was a forced 360 kilometer march in an effort to keep the prisoners from being liberated by the advancing Russian Army. During this time, the prisoners slept on the ground and received little to no food. At the end of this ordeal the guards surrendered those prisoners who survived the march, to American Army units.

The prisoners were flown to France and that is where Harold was when the war ended. He told of how there was little celebration. Everyone simply was glad the war was over. The men were occupied with recovering, having a full stomach and thinking of the day when they could go home.

That day finally arrived, and from France, Harold was sent to New York City where he caught a train for home. But his adventures weren't over yet. En route, the train on which he was riding, crashed near Milton, Pennsylvania. Eighteen people lost their lives and many others were injured. Harold miraculously survived, was credited with helping to pull many of the injured to safety, and was pictured in the local paper with a woman and her twelve-year-old son who he had rescued. However in the chaos of the wreck, he lost all his luggage and personal possessions. Nevertheless, happy to be alive, on a Friday evening in late June 1944, he finally arrived in Mayville with little more than the clothes on his back and the change in his pockets. Home to Fran, family and friends.

Harold was my father and surely an angel must have been watching over him, protecting him, keeping him from starvation, keeping him alive, making sure he survived not only the plane crash, but the train wreck, so he could return home to his beloved Fran.

44
Midnight Shift

Kaaren

My youngest son is a police officer, Head of Street Crimes. He works the mid-afternoon to midnight shift. After some planning it was decided that his unit plus the Swat team would go in and "take down" a crack house in a very unsavory neighborhood.

All was put into motion and about 11:30 at night the house was surrounded and my son was about to give the order to begin closing in.

About that time, I woke with a very unpleasant feeling and felt an urgent need to call him. This is something I rarely do because I feel when he is at work he should not be bothered unless it is extremely important. No one should be bothered at work for chit chat, especially if he has a job like my son's. However, the feeling was so strong that I got out of bed, found my phone and dialed his number.

As his phone rang and he saw my number he stepped back behind the prowl car, knowing I only call if it is important. Just as he did that a man burst out of the house shooting. The bullets hit the prowl car in the exact spot my son had been standing just seconds before.

Had he not moved, he probably would have been killed. The link between people can never be overlooked.

Love connects people. There is a definite force of Love that, when listened to, and that is the key, listened to, guides our lives.

45
A Light From Above

Marilyn

About three years ago, we received a lovely piece of sculpture from our friend, Howard who owned an art gallery. It is a beautiful, contemporary, colorful design in acrylic, created by a well-known Israeli artist.

Coincidentally, the sculptor is a distant relation to my husband who met him years ago when the artist came to Detroit for a show in an art gallery.

After Howard retired and closed his gallery, the lonely sculpture sat on a shelf in his garage for years, covered by an old towel. One day, he called us saying he wanted to give us one of the last pieces of art that remained from his gallery days because he was in his eighties and facing the time when he would need to enter an assisted living facility. He had Parkinson's disease, and it was progressing to the point where he knew he needed too much care to remain in his home any longer. He would have to sell it.

When he gave the piece of sculpture to us, he said he knew it would be in a happy home, and that would make him so glad. At the same time, we were delighted to acquire this beautiful piece of sculpture, had just the right corner for it, and bought a pedestal on which to place it. This colorful piece of acrylic is thirty-three inches high and can be lit from the pedestal below and a light in the ceiling above it. There is a small remote that we keep on a nearby table to turn these lights on and off.

Sure enough, less than a year after we bought the sculpture, Howard and his wife, Jennifer entered an assisted living facility. Sadly, Jennifer had Alzheimer's disease and needed a lot of help. They shared a little apartment together until Jennifer had to enter the Memory Care section of the facility. Howard spent every afternoon with her after that.

Every few weeks we would visit them and often Howard would ask if we were enjoying the sculpture. We assured him we loved it, which we do.

Sadly, we watched their health slowly deteriorate. Finally, in August 2015, Jennifer died. She had two sons from a previous marriage, but both tragically died in their forties, one from cancer and the other from a drug overdose. No grandchildren, no close relatives. All she had was Howard and he had promised his beloved Jennifer he would always take care of her, and this he did until the very end.

A few days after Jennifer died, I walked into the living room and found the light above the piece of sculpture was lit. I asked my husband if he turned on the light and he said, "I thought you did." I thought perhaps the cleaning lady had left it on for some reason, but she told us she never touched the light switch. Two days later, we found the light on again. This time we both agreed… Jennifer was sending a message that at last she was fine, free at last from the Alzheimers disease that stole her mind. After that, we found the light on one more time.

After Jennifer died, Howard had no purpose in life. Over the next two months, we visited him almost every weekend, and watched as he seemed to lose his will to live. His health rapidly worsened until one day, after not seeing him for about three weeks, we arrived at his room and were shocked to find him near death. He was in bed, eyes closed, a long narrow tube of oxygen extending from his nose. He could not speak, he could not move.

When we greeted him, he opened one eye, looked at us for a moment and shut his eye again.

No word.

No movement.

No acknowledgement that we were there.

Slowly, we realized he probably had suffered a paralyzing stroke. Two weeks earlier, he was fine and chatting with us and suddenly everything changed.

We knew this must be the end, the last time we would see him. It was time to say goodbye. My husband and I told him how he had been such a good friend all these years and how much he meant to us, that we loved him. We stayed a while longer in silence, said a prayer for him and then, tears in our eyes, quietly left knowing we would never see him again.

He died the next day.

The night after our visit with Howard, I thought I would turn on the light over the piece of sculpture; as a simple tribute. When I pressed the button on the remote, there was a flash from the light above. And then…no light…as if it had burned out. I stood there for a moment and thought, *Howard, it's you. You're gone. Your suffering is over. It's two months after Jennifer's death and now you have joined her. You're together at last.*

Three days later, we found the light on again. It hadn't burned out. This time it was Howard's turn to greet us.

Six months later, Howard's daughter held a memorial service for him in the garden of a lovely Bed and Breakfast. It was a beautiful day, the temperature was just right and there wasn't a cloud in the sky as his family and dear friends gathered to pay a last tribute to him. Later that day, the sky darkened and the gray clouds threatened rain, but during the tribute to Howard, the weather was perfect, as if the gallery owner had planned the perfect picture. The weatherman dared not interfere.

The night before the memorial service we found the light had mysteriously turned on again. Howard's last goodbye. Perhaps he wanted to tell us he was happy now that he had reunited with his beloved Jennifer. He was the love of her life and she was his. He called her his Queen of the Nile.

We don't think we will find the light mysteriously lit any more. We are sure they are too busy enjoying each other's company to bother contacting us anymore.

Request for Review

If you enjoyed this book,
please consider jotting a review about it on the
Marilyn Frazer book page at Amazon.com.

www.ingramcontent.com/pod-product-compliance
Lightning Source LLC
LaVergne TN
LVHW020634100826
845148LV00012B/2178

* 9 7 8 0 5 7 8 9 3 9 5 1 3 *